# Country House Cookery from the West

_Elizabeth Lothian_

DAVID & CHARLES

Newton Abbot    London    North Pomfret (Vt)

**British Library Cataloguing in Publication Data**

Lothian, Elizabeth
 Country house cookery from the West.
 1. Cookery, English
 I. Title
 641.5'9423      TX717

 ISBN 0-7153-7476-1

Library of Congress Catalog Card Number: 77-85035

First published 1978
Second impression 1979

Typeset by Ronset Ltd, Darwen, Lancashire
and printed in Great Britain
by Biddles Limited, Guildford, Surrey
for David & Charles (Publishers) Limited
Brunel House   Newton Abbot   Devon

Published in the United States of America
by David & Charles Inc
North Pomfret   Vermont 05053   USA

# CONTENTS

# ACKNOWLEDGEMENTS

The unfailing courtesy of those who have generously given of their time to contribute to this collection is acknowledged with gratitude. Members of the National Trust staff are thanked warmly for their willing and practical help. To Mary Lewis, Captain H. P. Chichester Clark and all the others who have given recipes or trusted me with precious country-house manuscripts and books, I am indebted and grateful.

The artist John Dyke is thanked for his complementary rôle, and the publishers for their attention and advice.

February 1977

# QUANTITIES AND CONVERSIONS

Quantities in the recipes in this book are given in both Imperial and metric units, and it is important to note that one or other system, *not* a mixture of the two, should be followed while using any particular recipe. In converting recipes the correct proportions must be maintained between liquid and dry ingredients.

The principal metric units used in this book are the kilogram (kg), the gram (g), the litre (l) and the millilitre (ml). Metric equivalents given in the recipes have taken 1oz to be approximately equal to 30g and 1 pint to be approximately equal to 600ml: these approximations mean that following the metric version of a recipe will result in 6% more. (Some cooks use 25g as the equivalent of 1oz and 500ml as the equivalent of 1 pint; these conversions give 10% less than when ounces and pints are used.) Should more accurate conversions be required at any point they are as follows:

| Metric | Imperial |
|---|---|
| 1kg (= 1000g) | 2·2lb |
| 0·455kg | 1lb |
| 1g | 0·0352oz |
| 28·35g | 1oz |
| 1l (= 1000ml) | 1·75 pints |
| 0·568l | 1 pint |
| 1ml | 0·0352 fl oz |
| 28·35ml | 1 fl oz |

The two main temperature scales used in cooking are the Fahrenheit and the Celsius (Centigrade) scales. The Celsius scale is defined by the melting point of ice, or, in effect, the freezing point of water, which is 0°C, and the boiling point of water, 100°C: on the Fahrenheit scale these temperatures are 32°F and 212°F respectively. We can see that therefore 180F° (212−32 = 180) equal 100C°, or, more usefully, 9F° = 5C°. So to convert from Fahrenheit to Celsius

5

subtract 32, multiply by 5 and divide by 9; and, similarly, to convert from Celsius to Fahrenheit multiply by 9, divide by 5 and add 32.

For example, $320°F = 160°C$ because

$$320 - 32 = 288,$$
$$288 \div 9 = 32,$$
$$\text{and } 32 \times 5 = 160.$$

The following scale gives useful approximations for oven temperatures:

|  | gas mark | °F | °C |
|---|---|---|---|
| very cool | $\frac{1}{4}$ | 225 | 110 |
|  | $\frac{1}{2}$ | 250 | 120 |
| cool | 1 | 275 | 135 |
|  | 2 | 300 | 150 |
| moderate | 3 | 325 | 165 |
|  | 4 | 350 | 180 |
| fairly hot | 5 | 375 | 190 |
|  | 6 | 400 | 205 |
| hot | 7 | 425 | 220 |
|  | 8 | 450 | 235 |
| very hot | 9 | 475 | 245 |
|  | 10 | 500 | 260 |

The Imperial measure today used in Britain superseded the Winchester measure and the Queen Anne Wine Gallon in 1824: however, accurate copies of these latter two standards had passed to the United States, were legally adopted in 1836 and still remain the standards there for dry and liquid measure respectively. Measurements given in this book in Imperial pints can be converted by using

1 US pint $= \frac{5}{6}$ Imperial pint ($= 16\cdot7$ Imperial fl oz)
and 1 US cup ($= \frac{1}{2}$ US pint) $= \frac{5}{12}$ Imperial pint.

The following tables of equivalents should prove useful:

*Liquid equivalents*

| Imperial | American |
|---|---|
| $\frac{1}{4}$ pint (1 English gill* | |
| $= 5$ fl oz) | $\frac{3}{5}$ cup |
| 8 fluid oz | 1 cup |
| 1 pint (20 fl oz) | $2\frac{1}{2}$ cups |
| 2 pints (1 quart $= 40$ fl oz) | 5 cups |

*1 Scottish gill $= 10$ fl oz.

## Equivalent weights of ingredients

| | |
|---|---|
| 1 oz yeast | 1½ cakes yeast |
| 1 lb flour | 4 cups flour |
| 8 oz sugar | 1 cup sugar |
| 8 oz butter | 1 cup butter |
| 4 oz chopped candied peel | 1 cup glacéed citron |
| 4 oz sultanas | ⅔ cup white raisins |
| 6 oz couverture chocolate | 6 squares bitter chocolate |
| 5 oz icing sugar | 1 cup confectioner's sugar |
| 16 oz maple syrup | 1½ cups maple syrup |
| gelatine 1 tabsp. | 1 envelope gelatine |

## Equivalent names for ingredients

| | |
|---|---|
| apple purée | apple sauce |
| apple (cooking) | apple (baking) |
| cornflour | cornstarch |
| digestive biscuits | Graham crackers |
| double cream | whipping cream |
| essence | extract |
| glacé cherries | candied cherries |
| icing | frosting |
| hard-boiled eggs | hard-cooked eggs |
| icing sugar | confectioner's sugar |
| plain flour | all-purpose flour |
| self-raising flour | all-purpose flour sifted with baking powder |
| single cream | coffee cream |
| sponge finger biscuits | ladyfingers |
| sultanas | seedless white raisins |
| tomato purée | tomato paste |

## ANTONY HOUSE
*Torpoint, Cornwall*

Sir John Carew Pole, Lord Lieutenant of Cornwall, gave the house and 29 acres of the immediate grounds (and later, further lands) to the National Trust in 1961; and he and Lady Carew Pole still live here. Lady Carew Pole was kind enough to allow us the use of these recipes for a meal which has been a family favourite.

The architect of this beautiful house, which was built between 1711 and 1721, is not known, but it is typical of its time and its style is echoed in the Radcliffe Camera at Oxford and St Martin-in-the-Fields in London. Inside, much is contemporary with the house, and fabric of 17th-century building remains. The original house first came into the possession of the Carew family in the 15th century and, as the *National Trust Guide* reminds us, 'No great house in the West Country is more vividly associated with Cornish history than Antony . . . Richard Carew . . . who succeeded in 1564, saw the Armada moving slowly up the coast . . . Despite the troubled times, his book and his portrait—both are still at Antony—reveal a serene and contented man.'

As with so many other great houses in the Southwest, turbulence and anxieties have raged through the centuries; but, again as with all of them, the tradition of public service by the owners and families has been maintained and today continues.

---

*Oeufs Weidel*
*Culotte de Boeuf*
*Profiteroles à l'orange*

## Oeufs Weidel

| | |
|---|---|
| 4oz (120g) long grain rice | 6 hard boiled eggs |
| about 8 fl oz (225ml) milk | Salt and pepper |
| Hollandaise sauce (see below) | Double cream |

Cook the rice in the milk, and when cooked add enough double cream to make a soft mixture. Season with salt and pepper and put into a gratin dish. Slice the eggs and put them across the rice. When the Hollandaise sauce is made, and the stiffly whipped whites added, spread this over the eggs. Place in the centre of the oven at 375°F (gas 5) and cook as for soufflé for 25 minutes. Serve at once.

### Hollandaise sauce

| | |
|---|---|
| Juice of ½ lemon | 1 dessertspoonful water |
| 3 egg yolks | 6oz (180g) butter |
| salt and freshly milled pepper | 4 stiffly whipped egg whites |

Put lemon juice and water into a small basin placed over a pan of hot water (or, if preferred, directly on gentle heat—in which case the process must be watched relentlessly!). Divide the butter into four parts. Add the egg yolks and one quarter of the butter to the liquid in the basin, and stir constantly and rapidly with a wire whisk over the hot (but not boiling) water until the mixture begins to thicken. Add the other three parts of butter one by one as each melts, whisking continuously. Remove from the heat and beat the sauce for 2 or 3 minutes until creamy. If it looks as though it might curdle beat a little cold water into it. Fold the stiffly whipped egg whites gently in, and complete the dish as above instructions.

9

## Culotte de boeuf

| | |
|---|---|
| 4½lb (2·2kg) rump steak | 2lb (960g) carrots |
| ½lb (240g) turnips | 1 large onion |
| a little white cabbage | ½ pint (300ml) brandy |

Marinade meat for two hours in the brandy. Put into a casserole with vegetables and about ¼ pint (150ml) water (and the marinade) and cook slowly. Cooking time for underdone meat, 30 minutes to 2½lb meat. Although the dish can be cooked longer the flavour is much better if served rare.

Slice the meat, put on a dish and surround with vegetables if desired.

## Profiteroles à l'orange

*For the choux pastry :-*

| | |
|---|---|
| 3¾oz (113g) strong plain flour | 1¼ gills (225ml) water |
| 2½oz (75g) butter | 3 eggs |

Sift flour with a pinch of salt, and put the bowl into a warm oven, just to warm the flour. Place butter and water in pan on gentle heat; when the butter has melted bring the water to the boil and draw aside. Tip the flour in, all at once. Beat until smooth and the mixture leaves the side of the pan. Add one egg immediately and beat again until smooth. Allow to cool a little and beat in the other eggs one at a time. Set oven to 425°F (gas 7). Shape mixture to the size of small eggs, or smaller; place the profiteroles on a greased baking tray and cook until crisp, about 30 minutes. Cut each profiterole in half, and put on a wire tray. When the caramel is ready, dip the top half of each of them into the caramel and leave to set.

## Caramel topping

| | |
|---|---|
| 3oz (90g) castor sugar | a little water |

In a small heavy pan put the sugar and water and cook slowly until it is a rich brown colour. (See page 73 for notes on caramel making.)

## Filling

| | |
|---|---|
| ¼ pint (150ml) cream | 1 orange |
| 4–6 lumps sugar | Approx. 2 tabsp. brandy |

Rub the lumps of sugar on to the orange to remove all the zest, then pound with a small amount of juice to make a thick syrup.

Whip the cream until thick, add syrup to it and stir the brandy into the cream. Fill bottom halves of the profiteroles with the cream, and place caramel-covered halves on top.

# ARLINGTON COURT

Arlington Court was given to the National Trust in 1946–7 by Miss Rosalie Chichester, whose family had owned the estate since the 14th century. The present house, designed by Thomas Lee in 1822, is delightful and full of interest. The stables house a large collection of horse-drawn vehicles, including those, or similar, used for the picnics described below. Dipper and Dapper and a young stallion occupy stalls here. Mr Jan Newman, who was with Miss Chichester and who until his retirement was Curator for the National Trust, has given me his time to share with me his enthusiasm for, and knowledge of, Arlington Court and its history, and I am truly grateful to him.

The restaurant at Arlington Court, as with the growing number of National Trust restaurants, maintains a high standard of good wholesome food, and a representative selection of recipes for dishes served there is included on page 24. The restaurant is in the kitchen of the house and is a light, attractive high-ceilinged place, with views through tall windows across lawns and trees. A single day is not enough to appreciate all that Arlington Court has to offer!

# Picnics at Arlington Court

Near Queen Victoria's Jubilee monument, where luncheon picnics were usually held, was pitched a Pavilion, or beautifully shaped tent, striped red, green and blue: it was lined, and the opening was draped back like curtains. There was a summer house here, too. Chairs were made of wickerwork with plaited seats, and could be folded away and stored in the summer house. The tables were low, made on the estate, with legs that unscrewed for easy storing.

For afternoon tea, Miss Chichester's favourite picnic place was by the summer house among the rhododendrons overlooking the lake, near where are today her memorial and grave, reached by way of the donkey walk. A donkey carriage made of wickerwork conveyed the picnickers, and the food and equipment were carried in a wooden donkey carriage. The luggage included a tripod camera and painting materials. Miss Chichester was accomplished in both these activities, as her remaining photographs and pictures, in both oils and watercolours show. Spirit lamp, kettle, boxes for tea and sugar, the special picnic china (white with gold bands) and tea napkins of fine damask were carried for afternoon tea. An afternoon tea picnic would include brandy snaps, plenty of iced cakes, sponge cakes, sandwiches of cucumber or egg, strawberries and cream, other fresh fruit—and, of course, tea.

As I have said, luncheon picnics were more usually taken at the monument on the hill, with views across the woods. Hot soups were conveyed in hay boxes. There were cold meats, cream caramels, fresh fruit, strawberry puddings and, for the guests, wine (Miss Rosalie Chichester never drank alcohol herself). Hot game soup, green salad (other salad ingredients such as radishes were assembled at the picnic), French dressing, rabbit brawn, home-made sausages, raised pies—all were made or prepared by Arlington's cook.

The following is an account of a picnic which took place in the summer of 1878, upon the return of the family from a cruise begun in 1877, as recalled to Mr J. Newman by Miss Rosalie Chichester.

On the family's return from Malta they put in at Southampton, where Sir Bruce Chichester, Miss Rosalie's father, normally laid up his yacht. Then, for the first and only time, they sailed on to Land's End and up to Ilfracombe. The yacht *Erminia*, a schooner of 276 tons, put in at Ilfracombe harbour where four carriages and the brake were waiting at the pier to take the visitors out to Arlington. There was to be a great picnic. On the way, other carriages joined until, arriving at the main Loxhore gates, there must have been thirty or forty carriages making their way up through the long drive to the house. Lunch was at 1 o'clock, and there was to be a cricket match in the afternoon.

The gentry made their way down to Swallowcombe Park (or Swallowcombe Meadow as it then was), overlooking the lake, where the picnic was laid out. The hot food was sent down in hay boxes, and the cold food kept in the Ice House at the top of the Wilderness until wanted. (At that time, ice came in as ships' ballast.) The menu included chilled game soup, veal rolls, fresh salmon, chicken in aspic, ham in aspic, cold baron of beef, salads, framboises à la crême, Adelaide trifle, strawberries and cream and ice puddings.

The match was played in the front park, where Sir Bruce had a first class cricket pitch. The estate employees played the gentry, among whom were Sir Bruce Chichester (Captain), the Chichesters from Shirwell (Youlston Park, the main branch of the family, founded in 1086AD, and Sir Francis Chichester's ancestors), the Chichesters from Hall, the Fortescues from Castle Hill, Mr Frere (a school friend of Sir Bruce), the Davies from Elms, Bishop Tawton, the Pines of East Down, and Lady Chichester's family, the Chamberlaynes of Cranbury Park, Hampshire.

---

### Rabbit brawn

*This recipe is from an Arlington cookery book of 1878 which was in continual use until at least 1920*

| | |
|---|---|
| 3 or 4 rabbits | chopped parsley |
| 4–6 eggs | chives |
| tomatoes | ¼oz (8g) gelatine |

Skin, clean, cut up and stew the rabbits in a little mutton stock until tender, but not over-cooked, having added salt and pepper. Take the meat from the bones and cut it into pieces. Put the bones back with the juices and boil gently for a half hour. Line a fairly large mould with a thin glaze, and sprinkle it well with chopped parsley. Lay the rabbit pieces in until about an inch from the top of the mould.

Boil the eggs hard, shell them and slice half of them to fill the top of the mould. Pour a little glaze over to set the eggs; leave in the ice box until set. Turn onto a fairly large dish. Carefully cut the rest of the eggs in half and remove the yolks and pass them through a sieve. Garnish around the turned-out shape. Fill the egg whites with parsley, yolks and chopped chives, and put a little glaze on each. Decorate with egg and tomatoes, sliced thinly. To make the glaze, take ½ pint (300ml) liquid from the stewed bones, etc., and add about ¼oz (8g) gelatine. For garnishing add a little more gelatine to the same amount of stock.

## Framboises à la crême

| | |
|---|---|
| 4oz (120g) sugar | 1lb (480g) fresh raspberries |
| gelatine | 3 whites of eggs stiffly beaten |
| 1 gill (150ml) cream | glacé cherries |

Boil the sugar in ½ pint of water until it becomes syrupy, then mix in the raspberries and allow them to cook slowly until the juice is extracted. Pass all through a sieve and leave to cool. Measure, and to each pint of purée allow 1½oz (45g) gelatine: dissolve this in a very little warm water, strain, and add to the purée. Add the cream and beat all together until quite thick. Stir frequently until it begins to set, then pile in the centre of a glass dish. Garnish with glacé cherries and plenty of whipped cream.

## Adelaide trifle

| | |
|---|---|
| macaroons | raisin wine |
| cold rich egg custard | ratafia drops |
| rich cream | whites of 3 eggs |
| sugar | grated lemon peel |
| raspberry jam | |

Lay the macaroons and ratafia drops on the bottom of a dish, and pour over as much raisin wine as they will soak up. Over this pour the custard, then the jam and cover the whole with the whip.

**The Whip**  Make this from the cream, whites of eggs, sugar, lemon peel, and raisin wine (or wine and lemon juice). Take approximately twice as much double cream as wine and about two tablespoonsful sugar, and grate the lemon peel. Stir the sugar into the liquid until dissolved. Continue to stir while the cream is slowly poured in. Beat until thick. Fold in the stiffly whipped whites of eggs, very gently. The mixture should be whipped very stiffly until it stands quite solid. Chill it overnight.

## Almond macaroons

8oz (240g) sugar                  4oz (120g) ground almonds
1 tabsp. rice flour (optional)      2–3 egg whites
Rice paper, non-stick baking paper, or lightly oiled trays

Mix dry ingredients, add egg whites and beat together for several minutes. Scrape from the sides of the bowl to mix thoroughly, and leave the mixture to stand for a few minutes. Beat again until thick and white. Shape neatly with two spoons, or pipe to make about 15 macaroons. Bake at 350°F (gas 4) for about 15–20 minutes. Remove from oven as soon as slightly coloured.

*The above recipes are from early Arlington manuscript books.*

---

## Ratafia drops or ratifies

*from Anne Andrews her book, a manuscript book of recipes begun in 1756*

1½oz (45g) bitter almonds and      3oz (90g) sugar sifted fine
1½oz (45g) sweet almonds*          1 white of egg
1 desp. brandy (optional)

Beat the almonds in a mortar and add the sugar, then the white of egg (and brandy, if used). Mix all together and drop it on paper. Make into about 25 small biscuits. Bake 5–7 minutes, 300°F (gas 2).

*Or 3oz (90g) sweet almonds altogether.

## Egg custard

*from Anne Andrews her book*

½ pint (300ml) new milk             1 desp. of pounded (castor) sugar
3 well beaten eggs

Dissolve the sugar in the milk and pour onto 3 well beaten eggs. Strain the mixture into a buttered basin which should be filled. Lay a sheet of buttered paper, then a floured cloth, over the basin and tye them tightly on. Boil the pudding gently for 25 minutes. Let it stand (if wanted for a shape) for 4 or 5 minutes more before turning out, or use it for the Adelaide trifle. If used as a shape serve wine sauce or spread jam round it.

# Arlington Court
# Menu

*Consommé*

*

*Filets de Soles*

*

*Mouton*
*Dindonneau rôti*
*Jambon*
*Pommes de terre      .      Celeri*

*

*Orange sponge*
*Mince pies*
*Salsify pie*


## Stock for consommé

| | |
|---|---|
| Meat bones, preferably marrow bones | 1 or 2 carrots |
| Poultry carcases, scraps and giblets | 1 bay leaf |
| 1 large onion stuck with cloves | 1 or 2 sticks celery |
| 12 peppercorns | small piece mace |
| 1 sprig marjoram | 2 teasps. sea salt |

Meat bones can be browned in a hot oven for a brown consommé.
Place all in a large pan, cover with cold water and simmer for as
long as possible—3 hours or more (this can be done in several
sessions). Cover with lid, not quite closed. Either leave until cold or
strain and put in a cold place until all fat has hardened and can be
lifted off and scraped clean. Boil the stock to reduce it and so
improve its flavour. Store in the freezer as ice-cubes: if stored in the
refrigerator it must be boiled every two or three days, or every day
if not.


## Beef consommé

| | |
|---|---|
| 1 onion and 2 cloves | 1 stick celery |
| 12 peppercorns | ½ bay leaf |
| sprig each thyme and marjoram | small piece mace |
| 1 glass dry sherry | 1 carrot |
| 4oz (120g) lean beef or shin | 2 egg whites |
| 3 pints stock, cold and skimmed | sea salt to taste |

17

Shred or mince the meat finely, prepare and chop the vegetables. Put everything except the sherry into a large pan, last being the egg whites stirred with a little cold water. Heat gently, whisking continuously, until the mixture just boils and a thick froth forms on the surface. Stop whisking, reduce heat until the liquid simmers; continue without boiling for about 20–30 minutes. Strain through double muslin or scalded jelly bag, ladling the mixture in so that the egg foam and its accretions are not disturbed. The consommé can be poured again through the egg whites' foam in the jelly bag or muslin. Return to a clean pan to reheat. Season and add a small lump of sugar and the sherry. Serves 4–6 persons.

### Fillets of sole

6 fillets of lemon sole
large cup of milk
lemon and parsley to garnish
fried breadcrumbs

salt, pepper
1 tablespoonful butter
1 desp. flour

Place the fish in a buttered fireproof dish. Add salt and pepper, and pour a large cupful of milk over. Cover and cook in a moderate oven for about 20 minutes or less. Lift the cooked fillets onto a serving dish, saving the liquor. Melt the butter in a pan and add the flour and blend. Add gradually, off the heat, enough liquor to make a sauce to coat the fish. Return to the heat and stir while boiling for two or three minutes. Garnish with lemon and parsley and fried-in-butter crumbs. Serve with thin brown bread and butter.

### Braised leg of mutton

A small leg of mutton
3 onions
a bunch of parsley
a few slices of bacon
½ pint (300ml) gravy or water

4 carrots
1 faggot savoury herbs
pepper and salt
veal trimmings

Line the bottom of a braising pan with a few slices of bacon, put in the carrots, onions, herbs, a bunch of parsley and seasoning and over these place the mutton. Cover the whole with a few more slices of bacon and the veal trimmings, pour in the gravy or water and stew *very* gently for four hours. Strain the gravy, reduce it to a glaze over a sharp fire, glaze the mutton with it, and send it to table placed on a dish of white haricot beans boiled tender, or garnished with glazed onions.

## Roast turkey

At 450°F (gas 7), cook approx. 15 minutes per lb, 35 minutes per kg (based on the weight of the prepared turkey), plus 15 minutes; or approx. 20 minutes per lb, 45 minutes per kg, when cooked more gently at 325°F (gas 3). Some recommend that after cooking for two thirds of the time the string tying the legs should be cut to ensure complete cooking. A cookery book contemporary with this menu advises that 'it is well basted the whole of the cooking time. About ¼ hour before serving, remove the [protective] paper, dredge the turkey lightly with flour, and put a piece of butter into the basting-ladle; as the butter melts baste the bird with it. When of a nice brown and well frothed, serve with a tureen of good brown gravy and one of bread sauce. Fried sausages are a favourite addition ... when these are not at hand a few forcemeat balls as garnish ... chestnut forcemeat with the chestnut sauce.' Boiled and roast potatoes, Brussels sprouts, bacon rolls and cranberry sauce are suitable as well, as is the braised celery mentioned in the menu.

### Chestnut stuffing for turkey
1lb (480g) chestnuts                    seasoning

Slit chestnuts, place in a saucepan and cover with boiling water. Boil for 10 minutes. Peel, skin and stew them in stock for about 10 minutes. Wipe the inside of the turkey with a damp cloth, and pack in the chestnuts, sprinkled with seasoning.

### Breadcrumb stuffing
8oz (240g) breadcrumbs                  ½ pint (300ml) milk, boiling
Turkey liver                            1 tabsp. chopped onion
chopped parsley and other herbs         seasoning
a little brandy (optional)

Put the breadcrumbs in a basin and pour the boiling milk over them. Leave to stand for 10 minutes. Mince or finely chop the liver with the onion and herbs, and add to crumbs and milk. Pack this stuffing into the neck end and draw flap over and attach firmly with skewer to the back of the bird.

### Orange sponge
1oz (30g) gelatine                      4–6oz (120g) sugar
4 oranges                               1 lemon
1 white of egg                          ½ pint (300ml) boiling water

Dissolve the gelatine in the boiling water, strain onto the sugar and add the juice of the 4 oranges and the lemon. When cool, add the white of egg slightly beaten. Whisk it until it becomes a stiff froth. Either pile it roughly in a glass dish, or before it is quite stiff put it into a wet mould.

### Salsify pie

| | |
|---|---|
| Salsify | 1oz (30g) butter |
| ½ pint (300ml) milk | 1oz (30g) flour |
| Anchovy essence | breadcrumbs and a little extra butter |

Wash and cook salsify for 10–15 minutes, when it should peel easily. Cut into pieces and boil until tender. Drain. Make anchovy sauce by melting the butter and flour together in a pan, adding the milk gradually and then the anchovy essence to taste. Put the salsify into a buttered fireproof dish, cover with the anchovy sauce and top with breadcrumbs and dabs of butter. Bake for 15–20 minutes in a moderate oven.

This recipe was given by Mrs J. Royle, whose aunt was Miss Rosalie Chichester and whose father was Rector of Shirwell, near Arlington. Mrs Royle remembers having this pie in childhood for Sunday supper after evensong. She grows salsify in her east Devon garden.

Although Eliza Acton wrote in her 1861 edition of *Modern Cookery* 'we are surprised that a vegetable so excellent as this should be so little cared for in England', there are continued references to it in cookery books; and the weekly journal *Garden*, in its issue of 11 November 1882, declared that 'salsify, when boiled in milk or fried in butter, has a peculiar resemblance to oyster'. Eliza Acton adds: 'Scorgonera is dressed in precisely the same manner as the salsify.'

# Arlington Court
# Menu

*le 6 juin 1906*

*Julienne consommé*
\*
*Saumon*
*Sauce Hollandaise*
\*
*Noisettes de mouton*
*Canetons*
*Petits pois*
*Asperges en branche*
\*
*Meringues*
*Beignets de bananes*
\*
*Balles de Parmesan*

## Julienne consommé

Use a good, cleared stock. Cut very fine strips of young carrots, celery, celeriac, and other suitable vegetables. Cut the strips about 1½in (4cm) long, and cook in a very small amount of the cleared stock. Add to the heated consommé.

## Salmon

Method as for salmon trout (page 56).

## Hollandaise sauce

*a 1906 recipe*

| | |
|---|---|
| ½ teasp. flour | 2oz (60g) butter |
| 2 tabsp. vinegar | 4 tabsp. water |
| the yolks of two eggs | the juice of ½ lemon |
| salt to taste | |

Put all the ingredients except the lemon juice into a stewpan. Set it over the fire and keep continually stirring; do not allow it to boil. Remove from the heat when the mixture is thick. Gradually add lemon juice.

21

## Dutch sauce

*from Eliza Acton*, Modern Cookery (*1861*)

| | |
|---|---|
| 3 egg yolks | the juice of a large lemon |
| 3oz (90g) butter | a little salt and nutmeg |
| a wineglassful of water (4 tabsp.) | a little cayenne |

Put all into a small saucepan. Keep the sauce stirred until it *almost* boils: a little cayenne may be added.

The safest way of making all sauces that will curdle if allowed to boil is to put them into a jar (or bowl) and set this over the fire in a saucepan of very hot water, then stir the ingredients constantly until the sauce is thickened sufficiently to serve.

## Noisettes de mouton

Best end of neck of mutton or lamb (6 noisettes in each)

| | |
|---|---|
| 3 tomatoes | 3oz (90g) mushrooms |
| fried croûtes | 2oz (60g) butter |
| seasoning | parsley |

Have the meat boned and rolled. Trim it and cut into $\frac{1}{2}$in (1cm) slices. Bat them out, season and fry them in butter over a brisk heat. Cut pieces of bread to fit each noisette, fry the bread in butter and then set a noisette on each piece. Carefully fry slices of tomatoes. Chop the mushrooms, fry them, and when ready to serve place a slice of tomato on each noisette, a little heap of chopped mushrooms on top and a little chopped parsley on each. Pour some Madeira sauce round and serve.

## Madeira sauce

### (a) brown sauce

| | |
|---|---|
| 1 pint (600ml) stock | 1 carrot |
| 2oz (60g) butter | 1 onion |
| 1½oz (45g) flour | seasoning |

Melt the butter in a pan, and put the sliced vegetables on to fry until dark brown—but not burnt. Stir in the flour and fry until it is a light brown, then add the stock and stir until it boils. Let the mixture simmer for 10 minutes. Season and strain through a hair sieve or tammy.

**(b) tomato sauce**

2lb (960g) tomatoes
6 peppercorns
1 small onion
1 small carrot
salt

2oz (60g) lean ham
½oz (15g) cornflour
1oz (30g) butter
1 sprig thyme

Peel and cut the onion and carrot into slices and chop the ham. Melt the butter in a saucepan and put in the vegetables and the ham; let them cook a little, then add cut-up tomatoes, thyme, peppercorns and salt. Simmer for ten minutes and then sieve. Blend the cornflour with a little cold stock or water, add to the reheated sauce and boil for two or three minutes, stirring. (A lump of sugar and some basil can be added.)

For the final sauce, take 8 fl oz (240ml) tomato sauce and 12 fl oz (360ml) brown sauce and simmer them together with 1 glass madeira or sherry for several minutes to reduce to a good consistency.

## Canetons

1 young duck* or number required

Prick the skin. Cover with buttered paper. Cook in a quick oven for about 1–1½ hours, according to size. When underdone, the juices run pinkish when the duck is pierced; when well done, clear yellow. Serve with green minted peas and asparagus.

*A caneton is a duck under six months old.

## Meringues

3 whites of egg                    6oz (180g) castor sugar

Whisk egg whites until they are stiff enough to hold a peak. Fold in sugar carefully. Lightly grease greaseproof paper or baking tins. Shape the whites with two dessertspoons and place in a very cool oven to dry out. When they can be moved about they are ready. This makes about 16–18 shells. Fill pairs of the shells with whipped cream prior to serving.

## Beignets de bananes

3 firm ripe bananas                batter
frying fat                         sugar

23

Cut each banana in half lengthwise, then each in half across. Dip the pieces in batter and then fry a golden brown. Drain, sprinkle with sugar and serve on a napkin on a hot dish.

**Batter**

| | |
|---|---|
| 4oz (120g) flour | ¼ pint (150ml) tepid water |
| a pinch of salt | 1 tabsp. salad oil or butter |
| 2 whites of egg | 1 yolk of egg |

Sieve flour and salt into a basin and add the yolk of egg, mixing it in with a wooden spoon. Then add the oil (or the melted butter) with tepid water: stir into the flour by degrees until a smooth paste is obtained, then beat for ten minutes. Leave to stand for half an hour or longer. When ready to use, whisk the whites to a stiff froth and mix in lightly.

**Balles de Parmesan**

| | |
|---|---|
| 2 egg whites | 2oz (60g) grated Parmesan cheese |
| salt and cayenne | |

Beat the egg whites to a stiff froth. Stir in the grated Parmesan cheese with salt and cayenne pepper to taste. Shape the mixture into balls the size of marbles, and drop them into very hot fat. Cook about five minutes until golden brown, drain well and sprinkle further grated cheese over them.

---

# The National Trust Restaurant

### Arlington chicken and ham loaf

| | |
|---|---|
| ½ pint (300ml) white sauce | 1¼lb (600g) cooked chicken |
| 4oz (120g) chopped onion | 4oz (120g) cooked ham |
| 4oz (120g) button mushrooms | 4oz (120g) white breadcrumbs |
| 2 tabsp. parsley | ¼ teasp. dried sage |
| salt and pepper | |

Mince chicken and onion, ham and mushrooms and stir into white sauce together with breadcrumbs and herbs. Season well. Line a 2lb loaf tin with foil and turn mixture into it. Cover with foil and place tin in a baking pan containing about 1in (2·5cm) of cold water. Cook at about 350°F (gas 4) for 1¾ hours. Cool in the tin. Chill and serve with a suitable salad; e.g., cold savoury rice or parsleyed tomatoes.

## Sweet and sour pork

3 tabsp. Worcester sauce
1 tabsp. grated orange peel
1lb (480g) pork tenderloin
salt and pepper

1oz (30g) butter
1 fl oz (30ml) oil
1 tabsp. sultanas
chicken stock

Into frying pan place 1 tabsp. Worcester sauce, and heat until it has almost disappeared; then add butter and oil. Cut pork into small cubes, add these and fry lightly. Place in a casserole. Cover with chicken stock, add 2 tabsp. Worcester sauce, orange peel and sultanas. Cook in medium oven for about one hour. Serve with apple sauce and vegetables.

## Junket (Devonshire style)

1 pint (600ml) fresh milk
2 teasp. Stone's rennet

2 tabsp. sugar
clotted cream

Heat 1 pint (600ml) milk to blood heat and dissolve 2 tabsp. sugar in it. Add 2 teasp. Stone's rennet. Allow to cool in room temperature. Serve with clotted cream.

A traditional way was to put some brandy in a bowl, then make the junket as above and place clotted cream over all.

# CASTLE DROGO
*Drewsteignton, Devon*

'... This romantic concept was splendidly fulfilled after twenty years of steady work,' wrote the author of a National Trust leaflet describing briefly the rooms which visitors see. At the end of the tour the visitor is advised 'on leaving the Chapel, to turn right, into a further tunnel under the main part of the house, to emerge on the east side. Turn right again and walk a short distance on to the promontory below the South Tower. There are dramatic views over the Teign gorge and on to the eastern flank of Dartmoor. The views of the long east façade of the house . . . are dramatic.'

You will come, there, with delight to the comfort of the restaurant for lunch, coffee or a traditional Devon Cream Tea. All is delicious, and the relaxation helps you to restore your sense of proportion after the mental effort of trying to compass the massive task of creating a castle in the 20th century (or any century, for that matter). If you can, go to Drogo when the Castle is full of flowers.

# The Flower Festival, 1976

The magnificent Flower Festival at Castle Drogo, to celebrate which this dinner was held, was co-ordinated by Mr Jack Woodrow. Preparations lasted for a full year. Each arrangement was carefully thought out and executed to suit its location; for example, the pillars leading into the drawing room had 12ft-high decorations of orange lilies and red roses. The castle during those days sang with colour, and the standard throughout was superb. Some of the most expert flower arrangers, including national demonstrators, gave their time for this occasion.

Mr Jack Woodrow was the National Trust Administrator at Arlington Court from 1949 to 1974, when he and his wife Ida retired to live at Broad Clyst—as did Mr Jan Newman, whom we have already mentioned in connection with Arlington Court. Mrs Woodrow, among a host of other duties, developed the shop at Arlington. She spent many hours caring lovingly for the precious christening gowns and the beautiful bed linen with its hand-made lace, and undertook many other tasks needing patience and skill. Mr Woodrow arranged the flowers at Arlington Court, and soon many visitors came for the sole purpose of seeing his beautiful, sensitively and imaginatively arranged flowers, which he had grown himself.

## Castle Drogo
## Flower Festival Dinner Menu

## 26 June 1976

*Fresh salmon mousse*

\*

*Roast Venison*

\*

*Fresh fruit salad*

\*

*Cheese*

\*

*Vintage port*

## Fresh salmon mousse

8oz (240g) fresh salmon
4 teasp. gelatine, dissolved in a
   little hot water
3 fl oz (90ml) mayonnaise

1 tabsp. lemon juice
⅓ pint (225ml) double cream
seasoning to taste

Bake the salmon gently in a little white wine, and flake when cold. Add seasoning and mayonnaise. Whip the cream and fold into the mixture, and add the gelatine and lemon juice. Pour into wetted mould or moulds, and allow to set. Serve, with thinly sliced brown bread and butter, on a lettuce base garnished with lemon and parsley.

## Roast venison

2–3lb (1–1½kg) venison, hung to
   personal taste
4oz (120g) red cherries, fresh,
   halved and stoned

one glass red wine
vegetable oil
vegetables to accompany

Brush the venison liberally with oil and place on a sheet of foil in a roasting tin. Pour the wine over it and wrap foil over the joint. Roast in a medium oven until tender, but do not overcook. Use all the meat juices for the sauce, thickening with a brown roux (1oz (30g) flour, 1oz (30g) butter or dripping, cooked together until a good colour is achieved). Boil the mixture, with cherries added, then simmer for five minutes. Pour sauce over the joint just prior to serving. Offer redcurrant jelly.

This was accompanied by new potatoes, garden peas, braised celery hearts and braised red cabbage.

## Fruit salad

Use apples, pears, pineapple, grapes, cherries and oranges; apples and pears can be prevented from discolouring by being dropped into an ascorbic acid solution immediately after being peeled and cut. Make a syrup 24 hours before required by boiling 11oz (330g) sugar in 1 pint (600ml) water. Prepare fruit and add to the syrup. Serve chilled and hand cream separately.

## Peppermint creams

1lb (480g) icing sugar
6 drops (or less) of oil of
   peppermint or peppermint essence

2 egg whites

Sieve the sugar if necessary. Place in a bowl and add the peppermint flavouring and the unbeaten egg whites. Mix and knead until a thick creamy paste is made. Wrap the rolling pin in greaseproof paper, sprinkle icing sugar on a small flat surface, and roll the paste to a thickness of $\frac{1}{4}$in (5mm). With a small cutter make shapes about the size of a florin. Leave to dry for several hours, and store between waxed papers in boxes. This makes about 6 dozen.

# COMPTON CASTLE
*near Paignton, South Devon*

You must go quietly to Compton Castle to hear the sounds of centuries past. The Gilbert family has lived within these 600-year-old walls through anxious, frightening, peaceful times; for the women, frequently lonely times.

The *National Trust Guide* tells us that 'when the great Tudor mansions were going up all over England, the Gilberts tended to be otherwise engaged'; for example, Sir Humphrey Gilbert's claim to immortality rests on his taking possession of Newfoundland for Queen Elizabeth in 1583, thus creating our first Colony. The late Commander Gilbert, in his National Trust publication, *Compton Castle*, described how Sir Humphrey was lost on the way home in his little vessel, the *Squirrel*, named after the family crest. It was around midnight on 9 September 1583, in the longitude of the Azores, that those in the *Golden Hinde*, who had entreated him to go in their larger vessel, saw the *Squirrel*'s lights go out. They had seen him earlier that day in the gathering storm, sitting abaft the mast with a book in his hand, giving signs of joy and calling out as

30

often as they approached within earshot, 'We are as near Heaven by sea as by land.' But he had told them, 'I will not forsake my little Company going homeward, with whom I have passed so many storms and perils.' The *Golden Hinde* survived to bring the news and, as Sir Winston Churchill wrote in his *History of the English-Speaking Peoples*, 'the first great English pioneer of the West had gone to his death'. He is the epitome of the Elizabethan age. In his home at Compton Castle is the only known authentic portrait of him.

'The Castle was restored, and the Hall completely rebuilt by Commander and Mrs Walter Raleigh Gilbert in the years between 1931 and 1956. That this was necessary can be judged by reference to the illustrations of the north front in the year 1900.'* Only a few rooms in the East wing were occupied, 'the West wing was left to become a ruin with neither roof nor woodwork of any kind, nor any glass in the windows, but with a great growth of ivy smothering it all. It was in that condition that Commander Gilbert, then a cadet on the way to HMS *Britannia* at Dartmouth, first saw the property in 1904.' But not until it came onto the market in 1930 was he able to secure it and the immediately surrounding land, once again for his family: '. . . the West wing, whose five fifteenth-century fireplaces were intact, was restored and made fully habitable.'

American visitors are deeply moved by Compton Castle and its close links with their country. Among all the other activities of the bicentennial year, 1976, a service was held in the Chapel during which a plaque was unveiled and dedicated. The plaque was presented by the Maine Society of Daughters of the American Colonists, and representatives from Maine were present.

Extracts from two articles printed in the *Journal Herald* of Ohio, September 1965, express very well both the American appreciation of Compton Castle and the sources of the feeling of cordiality that this fortified home offers.

> How must it feel to live in a Castle today? To climb the same spiralling stone steps and occupy the same rooms in which one's ancestors have lived and died for 600 years? To warm oneself before the same great fireplace that warmed the contemporaries of Chaucer, Shakespeare, Henry VIII and Sir Walter Raleigh?

and

> . . . the heavy oak door behind the portcullis entrance stood

---

*This and the following extracts are from Commander Gilbert's booklet, *Compton Castle*.

ajar and I stepped into the paved courtyard that gives entrance to the Great Hall, the Chapel and the Steward's Room ... How did it feel to stand there, in a timeless moment between the past and the future? Strangely enough I felt as though I, too, had come home. The great history of the English-speaking peoples, which until now had been only an uncertain dream pieced together by school books, at last took the form of solid continuing reality ... One gets the impression that Compton has continued to live and develop gracefully out of its past into its future—a far more seemly thing than structures that have been killed by their static preservation to a certain period. Because Compton is still alive its past seems more alive as well ... My other impression was that the living rooms were far more warm and light than I had expected, so pleasantly liveable as one could want.

There is a walled garden at Compton Castle, so peaceful during sunny summer days that it seems permanently set for tea. Imagine it in June, as it is now as I sit here in the shade of a large cherry tree. Before me is the rectangular pool in which swim goldfish among the leaves of waterlilies, now in full bloom, pale pink and pale yellow; bright large dragonflies skim across the water. Beside me, a huge philadelphus in full flower fills the corner of the garden, and cultivated foxgloves blossom in its shade. Pinks sprawl onto the grass from the edge of the herbaceous border, where the delphiniums and other perennials lift their flowers. On the left a stone pergola frames this garden and, clearly in its 'right' place, a large-flowered clematis, Nellie Moser, is in full bloom; later, roses will flower there. Beyond is the great curtain wall and the Castle. Here in the garden, in the centre of the flower border on the right, is a small terrace, approached up one or two steps, set in a bower of red roses with a well-established fragrant *Magnolia Wilsonii* on either side, and there is the small table for afternoon tea among all this fragrance. A slight breeze stirs, and in the quietness each tree and shrub makes its own distinguishable sound.

There are at least twenty-five varieties of camellias at Compton Castle, and nine different kinds of magnolia. Mrs Gilbert, whose exquisite paintings adorn her home, paints in watercolours flowers from the gardens, but particularly the camellias, paeonies and the magnolias.

Whether tea is here in the walled garden or, if the wind is high, in the courtyard, one factor is constant—Compton Scones. Commander

Gilbert used often to prepare these and the fruit cake, for both of which he was good enough to give the recipes; and he gave me also the recipe for one of his father's favourite dishes.

―――――――――

## Compton scones

*'These are very simple, but seem to have a good reputation among our friends from America.'*

4oz (120g) Marriage's 81 %
  self-raising flour
12oz (360g) white self-raising flour
1 heaped teasp. Royal Baking
  Powder (optional)
about 9½ fl oz (300g) milk,
  sour if possible

a pinch of salt
4oz (120g) butter

Mix flour, baking powder (if used) and salt in a basin. Work the butter into the flour between fingers and thumb, and when thoroughly absorbed add the whole of the milk, at once, and stir with a large wooden spoon. When the resulting dough is capable of being rolled on a floured board, roll it out to about ½in (1cm) thickness. Cut into rounds 2½in (6·5cm) in diameter and cook for 14 minutes in the oven at approximately 450°F (gas 8).

It is desirable to do the whole operation at speed. The scones should be slightly browned on top if the temperature and time have been right; this will be a matter of experience with one's own oven. Serve hot with butter and honey or jam.

## Fruit cake

8oz (240g) sugar
12oz (360g) self-raising flour
6oz (180g) sultanas
small pinch salt

8oz (240g) butter
4 eggs
2oz (60g) cut peel

Cream butter and sugar with a large fork in a basin. When thoroughly creamed, add the flour and the well beaten eggs alternately, at the rate of about one quarter of each at a time. When thoroughly mixed, add the sultanas and peel and mix again for a minute or two. The above quantities will require an 8in (20cm) tin; for a 6in (15cm) diameter baking tin, use half quantities. Bake at 375°F (gas 5) for 1½ hours, or, for the smaller size, 1¼ hours. Cover with a loose piece of brown paper or double grease-proof paper after 45 minutes' baking.

## Commander Gilbert's father's pears

6lb (2kg 880g) pears, weighed    a few cloves
   after having been peeled and cored  1 large wine glass of brandy
4½lb (2kg 160g) loaf sugar
optional red colouring
½ pint (300ml) port

Put the sugar into a preserving pan with enough water to wet it. Simmer until clear. Put the pears and cloves in and cook slowly until tender. Add wine, brandy and enough cochineal (if used) to colour. Keep in an earthenware jar with a cover, but do not seal. Enjoy them round about Christmas time.

## COTEHELE
### *St Dominick, Cornwall*

Sheltered by woods and above the steep banks of the Tamar . . .
rise the grey granite walls of Cotehele. This highly romantic
house is among the most authentic surviving examples of a
knightly dwelling built in the late medieval tradition. William
Edgcumbe, who married the Cotehele heiress, took possession
of this delectable place in 1353. Cotehele House was built
1485–1627 on the foundations of the earlier house. The Edgcumbe family left this house before the end of the 17th century,
to live in a . . . mansion, Mount Edgcumbe, and the remote
house above the Tamar was left much to itself . . . the Tudor
buildings thus remained . . . unaltered, and Cotehele acquired
the tranquil atmosphere, the sense of time distilled, that is so
striking.

(The *National Trust Guide.*)

The wonderful Great Hall at Cotehele reminds us of the times
when the lord of the house and the whole household banqueted

daily together. Later the Great Hall became the centre of ceremonial activities and public reception, and gradually meals began to be taken privately by the family in smaller rooms—dining, parlour, breakfast and nursery apartments.

Sadly, the house-books for Cotehele were destroyed in the war; but from other sources it is possible to describe the food that the busy kitchens would have provided when the house was lived in. We have many books from early centuries covering food preparation, dietary advice and medicinal remedies; every great house had its house books, and Cotehele's must have been interesting, spanning as they did, the upheavals of the Plantagenet times and the developing nation, until the tremendous thrust of Elizabethan times and overseas growth and expanding trade.

> Shall we know again days when wine and oil are plentiful, or have such glories gone, like the past, for ever? Much can be said in favour of modern kitchens. Will they degenerate into mere cubby-holes in which to heat the dull contents of tins, jars and cardboard boxes? Or can a lean era, which has made us properly aware of the pleasures of eating, stimulate the art of cooking in the future, that our tables will reflect triumphs greater than those of the Past?
>
> John Hampson, *The English at Table*, Collins (1946)

## Cornish pasty

home-made shortcrust pastry, made from 8oz (240g) flour
4oz (120g) margarine and vegetable shortening mixed
salt and pepper

8oz (240g) pasty beef, chuck steak
2 medium potatoes
small swede (optional)
1 medium onion

The quantities given make two pasties. Roll out pastry in two rounds to size of side plate. Put potato and swede (diced or chipped very small) in centre of pastry and add pepper and salt. Cut meat into very small pieces and place on top of vegetables; add chopped onion on top. Sprinkle a teasp. of flour over top and season again. Finish with small knob of butter. Damp edges of pastry and bring together over the top, crimping as you go. Make small slit in the top for steam to escape and brush with egg and milk. Bake at 450°F (gas 8) for 20 minutes, and at 300°F (gas 2) for a further 40 minutes.

The dedicated Cotehele cook of many years' standing explained that the 'crimping' of the pastry can only be learned from a Cornish (or Devonshire) cook.

## Pork and apple in cider

| | |
|---|---|
| half a boned and rolled leg of pork | 2 green peppers |
| 8oz (240g) tin of tomatoes | 1 large onion |
| 4oz (120g) sliced mushrooms | 2 large cooking apples |
| 1 pint (600ml) cider (preferably farmhouse) | |
| seasoning | |

Remove excess fat and dice meat. Fry meat in a little oil until brown, and drain off fat. Sweat mushrooms, peppers and onion in butter until golden brown. Put meat, vegetables and cider in a casserole and cook until tender. Peel and core apples and cut into rings; brown these in a little butter and add to the casserole a few minutes before serving. If liquid needs thickening add a little flour mixed with stock, and simmer until sufficiently thick. Sprinkle with chopped parsley and serve with baked potatoes and green salad.

## Fresh fruit and cream gâteau

| | |
|---|---|
| 3 eggs | 6oz (180g) castor sugar |
| 6oz (180g) self-raising flour | ¾ pint (450ml) whipping or |
| fresh fruit (failing that, canned) | ½ pint (300ml) double cream |

Beat eggs and sugar until thick and creamy (about ten minutes) and fold in the well-sifted flour. Pour into greased and floured deep cake tin of 8in (20cm) diameter and bake for 40 minutes at 325°F (gas 3). When cool, cut cake carefully into three layers. Use half cream and fruit for the filling, and pipe the remainder of the cream on top of the cake and decorate with fruit.

———————

'This gâteau is made in Cotehele's kitchens by the ladies there, and it is very popular: it is a beautiful light sponge, very attractive to look at, and not expensive if fresh seasonable fruits (e.g., strawberries, raspberries, peaches, etc.) are used. Should serve 6–10, depending upon appetites.'

The pork and apple in cider 'proved to be one of Cotehele's most popular "hotpots" and was devised by one of Cotehele's chefs'.

# KILLERTON
*near Exeter, Devon*

Killerton Estate (5 miles north of Exeter on the A38) was given to the National Trust in 1944 by Sir Richard Acland, to whose family it had belonged for three hundred years. The chief glory of Killerton has always been the garden: its informal combination of trees, lawns and flowering shrubs, sheltered by the hill known as Killerton Clump, makes an attractive refuge—not only for visitors from afar but also for many people who live in Exeter and the surrounding neighbourhood. It is open all the year round, and there are very few days in any season when it is not possible to find some plant or shrub in flower. The house (rebuilt in 1777) fits well into its framework of park and garden, and now forms the administrative centre for the Devon Area of the National Trust. Visitors can go into the garden through the house, and perhaps recapture some of its former atmosphere. A restaurant, made out of the old billiard room and 'still-room' (where all the preserving for the house was once carried out), opens immediately on to the garden.

The Aclands themselves now live at the dower house, Sprydon,

38

at a little distance from Killerton. Lady Acland has contributed the following notes.

'No records of elaborate Acland entertaining remain to provide a source for interesting historical recipes and menus. Perhaps this is because the tradition of the family, for many generations, has been one of public work: one gets the impression that food has usually taken second place to politics. Certainly my own memories of meals in the 1930s (the time when Killerton was last lived in as a complete family house) are of suppers kept hot in the oven for people returning late from election meetings rather than of dinner-parties with inscribed menus. To be sure, there were family feasts at Christmas, when large numbers of relations assembled, and then the walled kitchen garden helped to supply their needs: wheelbarrows full of vegetables would be pushed up to the back door, and somebody now living and working at Killerton recalls that on one particular occasion 57 heads of celery were dug—by pick-axe—out of hard-frozen ground and barrowed up to the house in a single load.

'In the two recipes which follow, I have not attempted to recall past meals, but have related them strictly to the present day and the needs of my own family. The domestic deep-freezer is the modern equivalent of the Ice House (built in Killerton Garden, 1808, and filled with ice from ponds, to keep meat fresh: it can be seen above the Rock Garden), and I find recipes which do not require long thawing particularly useful.'

### Braised beef from the freezer

2–3lb (1–1½kg) beef (a neat joint of topside is ideal)
3 large onions
bouquet garni
butter for frying

a few large carrots
a little red wine
salt and black pepper

'Find a casserole which the meat fits without too much room to spare. Rub the *frozen* meat with black pepper, and fry it really dark brown in a little butter. Remove from the pan. Roughly chop the vegetables and fry them a rich colour, seasoning them *while they fry* with salt and pepper. Now, in the bottom of a casserole lay first the fried vegetables and then the meat and bouquet garni. Pour wine around, so as just to top the joint: there ought not to be much room for it. Home-made wine is very adequate: otherwise the cheapest possible. Cover the casserole with foil in addition to its own lid, to make a very secure seal, and put in an oven at 225°F (gas ¼) for 8 hours or overnight. It will be cooked when a skewer runs through the joint with no resistance at all. On the other hand, it should not fall to pieces, so careful testing is needed. When cooked, put the casserole in a cold place overnight, so that the fat forms a solid cap on top. *Remove this with scrupulous care.* Now take out the meat, and very carefully cut it into well shaped pieces across the grain, laying them as you do so in a clean casserole, suitable for serving. Discard anything in the way of gristle or membrane, so that every slice is completely edible. Remove bouquet garni from the cold gravy, and put the gravy through the blender. The vegetables will make the sauce beautifully thick, without additions, but check the seasoning and add a drop or two of gravy browning if this is necessary for an attractive appearance. The dish is now ready for gentle reheating (it needs no further cooking): 1–1½ hours at 210°F (below gas ¼) would be suitable. The secret of success is the *complete removal of fat*.'

### Frozen fool

| one 8 fl oz (240ml) carton | icing sugar |
|---|---|
| double cream | 2 egg whites |
| about 8 fl oz (240ml) frozen strawberry purée | |

'Whip cream fairly loosely, adding the (barely thawed) fruit purée and continuing to whip, so that it is nicely thick. Add a little icing-sugar, being careful not to over-sweeten. Whip egg-whites really stiff, and fold into the mixture. Spoon into a pretty dish and put into the ice compartment of the refrigerator for about two hours before it is needed. It should be beginning to solidify round the edge of the dish, but no more, so watch carefully. Serves four generously.'

---

'Two of our sons are working in America at present, and have converted us to the convenient custom of serving starters with the pre-meal drink, rather than at the dinner-table. Savoury 'dips' seem to be the prime favourites, and nowadays cookery books on both sides of the Atlantic include a choice of recipes for these succulent and creamy mixtures. However, it is hard to find recipes for biscuits

40

—or "crackers"—to use for the actual dipping: it is assumed that one can buy the firm "corn crisps", which are so suitable, as easily in England as in the States. This is not so, and ordinary potato crisps are no good at all as they fall to bits when stuck into the dip, and scatter mess everywhere. I invented the following recipe in a hurry, inspired by the sight of an unwanted packet of breakfast cereal left behind by one of the grandchildren.'

## Sprydon dip-crackers

4oz (120g) suitable fine-oat cereal     3 tabsp. single cream
pinch of salt

'Mix well, knead and roll out as thin as you can, sprinkling some dry cereal on the work surface and the rolling pin. Cut into diamond shapes with a cutter about 2in × 1½in (5 × 4cm) for easy dipping. Bake in the oven at 350°F (gas 4) for about 15–20 minutes until brown and crisp, watching carefully in case they burn.'

## Pre-prandial dip
soft full fat cheese and about one     double or single cream
    quarter of its weight in butter     lemon juice

'Beat all together until of a suitable "dipping" consistency. Season *very* carefully. Add from the following selection with discretion: chopped parsley, chives or other suitable fresh herbs; one or two drops of pressed garlic juice; a pinch of cayenne pepper; small pinch of curry powder; a few drops of Angostura aromatic bitters; celery salt.'

# KNIGHTSHAYES COURT
*Devon*

During an epilogue late one evening on BBC Radio 4 I heard a monk say that even inanimate objects, if cared for with affection, respond and reveal their inherent beauty. We know all living things respond to love and affectionate care, and there is no better example than Knightshayes gardens, which are truly beautiful.

Wide straight-edged walks do not constrain your travels through the gardens; you stroll gently along woodland paths which lead to places whose vistas cause you to stop with delight: they form, it seems, garlands held in place by trees of satisfying proportions.

Sir John and Lady Amory designed, arranged and planted these gardens themselves. Pre-war plans came to a standstill, and the gardens were developed during the thirty years after World War II. The deep woods were cleared of the tangled undergrowth, and bit by bit the fence was pushed back. The good trees were left standing, and the gardens formed round them. Gardens close to the house have been gradually improved. The high yew hedge once enclosed a bowling green which lay where the pool now is, brooded over by an elegant grey-leaved pyrus (*Pyrus salicifolia pendula*); this is a peaceful place. Maples of many varieties give grace and colour through the woods, and the latest addition, the willow garden, will in a few years be fully mature.

The following recipes from Lady Amory are 'meals we share with guests for parties'.

## Summer Lunch

*Country pie*
*Fresh peas*
*Mocha Gâteau*

\*

## Summer Sunday Supper

*Chicken and curried rice*
*Fresh fruit salad*
*Cream horns with Devonshire cream*

### Country pie

2oz (60g) flour
2oz (60g) butter
¼ pint (150ml) milk
½ pint (300ml) chicken stock
wineglassful white wine
a little cream

2oz (60g) cooked macaroni
2oz (60g) grated cheese
chopped-up cooked chicken
a little extra grated cheese

Line a pie dish with shortcrust pastry.

For the filling make a good white sauce. Melt the butter in a saucepan, add the flour, stirring all the time, and gradually stir in the milk and the chicken stock. Over a gentle heat bring to the boil. Add a wineglassful of wine and a little cream. The sauce should be nice and creamy.

Then add the macaroni (already boiled until quite tender), the cheese and finally the chopped-up cold cooked chicken. Fill the pie dish and cover with a little sprinkling of grated cheese. Bake in a moderate oven for about ¾–1 hour. Alternatively the pie can be covered with rosettes of creamed potatoes before cooking. Serve with fresh peas. To serve the pie as a supper dish, omit potatoes and, when cooled, decorate with slices of tomatoes and cucumber, and cover with aspic jelly.

## Mocha gâteau

1 sponge round, 7–8in (18–20cm)
3oz (90g) icing sugar
2 tabsp. concentrated black coffee
¼ pint (150ml) cream

3oz (90g) unsalted butter
2 well beaten egg-yolks
1 tabsp. rum or brandy
chopped toasted almonds

Cream butter and sugar, add egg yolks and coffee. Slice the sponge cake into halves and spread the mixture on one, covering with the other. Place in a round cake tin and put a plate over it (to fit *inside* the tin). Place a weight on top. Leave several hours so that the mixture may seep into the cake. Turn out, cover with ¼ pint (150ml) lightly whipped cream and sprinkle with chopped toasted almonds. 1 tabsp. rum or brandy may be added to the butter cream, and a little to the whipped cream for added flavour.

## Chicken and curried rice

1 young chicken
wineglassful of white wine or cider
6oz (180g) butter
1 pint (600ml) good stock

½ pint (300ml) double cream
1 teasp. Worcester sauce
1 teasp. curry powder
6oz (180g) Patna rice

Cut the chicken into 8–10 pieces, depending on size. Melt 3oz (90g) of the butter in a thick saucepan and, after seasoning the chicken, fry it in the butter until nicely browned on both sides. Put the lid on the saucepan and finish cooking slowly for about 30–45 minutes. When ready remove pieces and keep hot. Drain off a little of the butter in the pan, add the white wine or cider, stir well and boil for a few minutes to reduce. Add cream, Worcester sauce and seasoning. Put chicken back in the sauce and cook for a further five minutes. Serve with curried rice, prepared as follows.

Melt the remaining 3oz (90g) butter in another saucepan, add rice and fry until nicely browned. Keep stirring, then drain off excess fat, add curry powder and stock, season and cook with lid on rice until all liquid is absorbed (about 15 minutes). Stir occasionally with a fork. Arrange the chicken on a serving dish surrounded by the rice, which should be dry with each grain separate.

## Fresh fruit salad

Make a fruit syrup with about 4oz (120g) castor sugar boiled with 5–6 fl oz (150ml) water. Use any fresh fruit available—for example, apples, oranges, peaches, apricots and, to add colour, raspberries and strawberries. Prepare the fruit and cover it with the syrup. Accompany the fruit salad with cream horns made with puff or flaky pastry, filled with Devonshire cream.

## Autumn Lunch

*Sweet and sour pork*
*Apple Charlotte*

\*

## Autumn Dinner

*Beetroot soup*
*Devilled pheasant*
*Pommes Anna*
*Fresh vegetables*
*Biscuit ice*

### Sweet and sour pork

pieces of cooked roast pork, or belly of pork, boiled and roasted until crisp
2 medium sized peppers, cut up and fried in oil
small tin drained pineapple
long-grained rice
fried chopped onions

cooked carrots
soya sauce
4oz (120g) brown sugar
2 tabsp. tomato purée
little sherry
a little cornflour
an omelette, diced

Heat the peppers, pineapple, soya sauce, carrots, sugar and tomato purée together, then add the meat. Mix a little cornflour with a little sherry and add to the mixture. Bring all to the boil. Serve with long-grained rice garnished with fried chopped onions, diced omelette and, if you wish, green salad.

### Apple Charlotte

golden syrup
stewed apples
grated lemon rind and juice
a knob of butter

slices of bread dipped in melted butter
sugar
Devonshire cream

45

Put a layer of golden syrup in a mould, then line the mould with slices of bread which have been dipped in melted butter. Stew apples with grated lemon rind, the juice of a lemon, sugar and a knob of butter. Pour into the mould and bake in a moderate oven for about 30 minutes. Turn out and serve with Devonshire cream.

### Beetroot soup

| | |
|---|---|
| beetroots | stock |
| onion | dill or other herbs |
| seasoning | flour |
| red wine | cream |

Grate beetroot into saucepan, add stock, onion, dill or other herbs and seasoning. Cook then strain through a hair sieve. Blend some flour with red wine, stir into the soup and return to the heat to thicken it. Garnish with a blob of cream.

### Devilled pheasant

| | |
|---|---|
| 1 pheasant | a few bacon rashers |
| 6oz (180g) whipped cream | 1 tabsp. Worcester sauce |
| a little Tabasco | salt and pepper |

Roast the pheasant for 20 minutes per lb (45 minutes per kg) at 425°F (gas 7). Put bacon rashers on the breast or brush with butter or oil. Slice when cooked and place the slices in a flat baking dish. Coat with a cream made by mixing the remaining ingredients, and put into a moderate oven for 20–30 minutes. Serve with runner beans and Pommes Anna. (To make Pommes Anna, slice potatoes thinly, dip the slices in melted butter, put a few slices each in small patty pans and bake for about 20 minutes.)

### Biscuit ice

Make ice cream as described on page 51. Arrange layers of ice cream alternately with layers of digestive biscuits and cream, with brandy sprinkled on each.

# Winter Lunch

*Beef olives*
*Brussels sprouts*
*Potato croquettes*
*Toffee pudding*

\*

# Winter Dinner

*Grapefruit grilled*
*Chicken, pineapple and*
*sweetcorn pancakes*
*Fresh vegetables*
*Ginger cream*

## Beef olives

*for six people*

| | |
|---|---|
| 1½lb (720g) topside of beef (if necessary, sliced thinly by the butcher) | 1 tabsp. flour |
| | stock or red wine |
| | 1oz (30g) suet |
| 6oz (180g) breadcrumbs | 1 egg |
| parsley, thyme, grated lemon rind | seasoning |

Mix all the ingredients (except the flour, wine and beef) together and spread on each slice of beef. Roll and secure each with small skewers, silver if possible. Fry the beef olives and put them into a casserole, then stir a tablespoonful of flour into the frying pan, add stock or red wine, boil and pour over the olives enough to cover them. Cook in a moderate oven for about 1 hour.

## Potato croquettes

| | |
|---|---|
| cooked potatoes | egg yolk |
| beaten egg | flour |
| breadcrumbs | butter and oil for frying |

Cream the cooked potatoes, add egg yolk, and make small shapes. Roll these in flour, then into beaten egg, and finally into breadcrumbs. Fry in butter and oil.

47

## Toffee pudding

4oz (120g) butter
thick slices of bread
Devonshire cream

4 tabsp. golden syrup
4 tabsp. brown sugar

To m ke the toffee sauce, blend the butter, syrup and sugar together over gentle heat until the butter is melted. Remove the crusts from the slices of bread, and turn them over in the sauce. Leave for five minutes over very gentle heat. Place on a very hot dish and serve with Devonshire cream.

## Grilled grapefruit

Halve three grapefruit, sprinkle with brown sugar and grill. (This and the following recipe are for six people.)

## Chicken, pineapple and sweetcorn pancakes

4oz (120g) flour
$\frac{1}{4}$pint (150ml) milk
6 breasts of chicken
12 slices of pineapple
  (fresh or canned)

2 eggs
1 small tin sweetcorn
breadcrumbs
butter, oil and fat
flour for coating

To make the sweetcorn pancakes, beat the milk, flour and one egg together. Add enough sweetcorn to make a thick pancake mix. Heat a little fat in a pan and drop in enough mixture at a time to make pancakes of $2\frac{1}{2}$in (6cm) diameter.

Take the breasts of chicken and cut each into two neat portions. Beat one egg. Dip the floured chicken portions into it, then into breadcrumbs. Fry in hot mixed butter and oil until golden brown, then put in the oven at about 300°F (gas 2) until cooking is complete. Heat the slices of pineapple through in the oven.

Place each piece of chicken on a slice of pineapple. Serve on a single dish, with cauliflower or other vegetables—for example, leeks, baked parsnips—surrounding the pancakes and chicken.

## Ginger cream

4 eggs
4oz (120g) chopped stem
  ginger and syrup
$\frac{1}{2}$ pint (300ml) double cream

3oz (90g) castor sugar
ground ginger (optional)
$\frac{1}{2}$oz (15g) gelatine

Separate the yolks of the eggs from the whites, add the sugar to the yolks and beat until they are pale. Add the ginger and some syrup (and some ground ginger if desired). Take the double cream, having added to it the gelatine melted in hot water, and add this to the mixture. When almost setting add the stiffly whipped egg whites. Garnish with cream.

## Spring Lunch

*Lamb stew in cider*
*Fresh vegetables*
*Prune soufflé*

*

## Spring Supper

*Crab pancakes*
*Vanilla ice cream, walnuts*
*and maple syrup*

### Lamb stew in cider

loin of lamb (5–6 cutlets)          oil to fry
6 onions                            6 small carrots
1 turnip                            1 parsnip
bouquet garni                       cider
clove of garlic

The loin of lamb is chined and divided into cutlets. Fry them on both sides to seal, and put into a casserole. In the frying pan, fry sliced onions, carrots, turnip, one parsnip and add to the meat, with the bouquet garni or crushed garlic. Cover with cider and cook slowly for about 1–1½ hours. Serve from the casserole with fresh vegetables.

### Prune soufflé

1lb (480g) prunes                   4oz (120g) brown sugar
1 lemon                             3 eggs, separated
1 tabsp. icing sugar

Soak about 1lb (480g) prunes in cold water overnight; add 4oz

(120g) brown sugar and the rind of a lemon and cook until tender. Sieve half the prunes and stone the remainder. Put a thin layer of the purée in the bottom of a soufflé dish. In a basin put the rest of the purée with the yolks of three eggs and 1 tabsp. icing sugar, and mix. Whip the whites of the eggs very stiffly and fold them gently into the purée. Cook in a moderate oven for 15 minutes. Reduce the cooked liquor to about ½ pint (300ml), pour over stoned prunes and serve these separately.


## Crab pancakes

*for six people*

| Pancake Mixture | Filling |
|---|---|
| 4oz (120g) plain flour | 1 small onion |
| a pinch of salt | 1 small apple |
| 1 whole egg, 1 egg yolk | 1 heaped teasp. curry powder |
| ½ pint (300ml) milk | 1 desp. flour |
| 1 tabsp. olive oil | 1 small tin crab meat |
| 2 tabsp. brandy (if liked) | ½ cup velouté sauce |
| | butter for frying |

Sieve the flour into a basin with salt. Make a hole in the flour and drop in egg and egg yolk. Mix to a thin batter with the milk, adding olive oil and brandy. Let the mixture stand three or four hours, then make pancakes in the usual way.

Finely chop the onion and fry lightly in butter; finely chop the apple and fry this also. Add curry powder and flour, and mix well with a little milk to make a smooth paste. Cook for 2–3 minutes, then add crab meat and velouté sauce (see below). Fill the pancakes with this mixture, roll them and lay them in a fireproof dish. Sprinkle with Parmesan cheese and a few knobs of butter. Place under a hot grill to brown and serve very hot.


### Velouté sauce

| | |
|---|---|
| 1oz (30g) butter | 4 white peppercorns |
| a few parsley stalks | trimmings of white mushrooms |
| salt | ¾oz (25g) flour |
| ½ pint (300ml) white stock | a few spoonsful cream |
| juice of ¼ lemon | |

Melt butter, add peppercorns and parsley, then flour and cook for a few minutes without browning. Add stock slowly, stir until well boiled, add lemon juice, mushroom trimmings and salt. Simmer gently for 20 minutes, stirring often. Tammy the sauce or strain through double muslin, then reheat and add cream carefully. Use as required.

## Vanilla ice cream

½ pint (300ml) double cream
4 desp. castor sugar
chopped walnuts

4 whites of eggs
vanilla
maple syrup

Whip egg whites stiffly and add to double cream with 4 desp. castor sugar and so·ie vanilla. Freeze until ready. Serve with walnuts and maple syrup, handed separately.

---

# National Trust Tearoom

The National Trust restaurant at Knightshayes Court offers that great Devonshire attraction, Devonshire Cream Teas, as well as other delicious teatime specialities. The National Trust Staff has been kind enough to share some of the recipes for favourites that have been used in the tearooms.

## Scone mix

1lb (480g) self-raising flour
2 eggs
2 level tabsp. castor sugar
small pinch salt

2oz (60g) butter
2oz (60g) margarine
milk

Mix dry ingredients. Rub in the butter and margarine. Whisk eggs and milk together and mix with the dry mixture to a soft dough. Roll out and using a 2½in (6cm) cutter make about 18–20 scones. Bake in a hot oven, 425°F (gas 7).

## Chocolate mint cream shortbreads

8oz (240g) plain flour
2oz (60g) castor sugar
4oz (120g) plain chocolate covering

7½oz (225g) butter (or margarine)
a few drops of almond essence
3oz (90g) icing sugar
a few drops of peppermint essence

Cream sugar and 6oz (180g) butter until soft. Add the flour. Knead until free from cracks. Roll out. Using a 2½in (6cm) cutter, make the shapes. Prick the tops and bake in a slow oven (300°F, gas 2) for about 30 minutes, or until pale golden brown. When the biscuits are cool, sandwich them together in pairs with the mint-flavoured cream (see below). Melt the chocolate in a double saucepan (do not overheat it) and spread over the tops.

For the filling, beat together 1½oz (45g) butter, 3oz (90g) icing sugar and a few drops of peppermint essence until white and smooth.


### Knightshayes chocolate krisp

8oz (240g) or 1 small
  block of compressed dates
4oz (120g) butter
  (or butter and margarine)
1 desp. golden syrup

5oz (150g) milk chocolate
  couverture or cooking
  chocolate
4 cups Rice Krispies
1oz (30g) castor sugar

Break up dates and put with a little warm water over low heat to soften and become mushy. Add fat, sugar and syrup, and stir and mix over the low heat. Remove pan from the stove and mix in the Rice Krispies thoroughly. Put the mixture into a lightly greased Swiss-roll tin, and press down well. When it is cold, cover with melted chocolate, which should be heated very gently in a double saucepan. Cut into square pieces.


### Peanut cookie

4oz (120g) brown sugar
4oz (120g) fat (margarine or
  nut fat)
4oz (120g) peanut butter
6oz (180g) plain flour

4oz (120g) white sugar
1 teasp. bicarbonate of soda
1 egg

Add the soda to the flour, and rub the fat and peanut butter into this mixture. Add the sugar and the egg and mix well. Roll into balls the size of a marble and place 2in (5cm) apart on a greased tin, *or* put into a Swiss-roll tin and press well down. Bake for 20 minutes at 350°F (gas 4). Cut into squares while still hot, but leave to cool in the tin.

## Date and hazelnut crunch

8oz (240g) margarine
2oz (60g) golden syrup
3oz (90g) dates or raisins

8oz (240g) Demerara sugar
10oz (300g) rolled oats
4oz (120g) hazelnuts, chopped

Melt the margarine and add the sugar, golden syrup, rolled oats, chopped dates and chopped hazelnuts. Mix well, making sure, if dates are used, that they are soft and mushy. Put into a well greased Swiss-roll tin. Bake in a moderately hot oven (300°F, gas 2) for 20 minutes or less until brown: do *not* overcook or it will become too hard. Allow 5 minutes to cool before cutting into squares.


## Spicy fruit cake

4oz (120g) sultanas
2oz (60g) cut mixed peel
1oz (30g) chopped almonds or
    walnuts
½ level teasp. mixed spice
8oz (240g) self-raising flour
5oz (150g) castor sugar

4oz (120g) currants
2oz (60g) chopped glacé cherries
1 level teasp. cinnamon
2 large eggs
5oz (150g) butter or margarine
3 fl oz (90ml) milk (approx.)
small pinch of salt

Cream the butter and sugar until the mixture is light. Beat the eggs and add to the creamed mixture with a little flour. Sprinkle some of the flour over the fruit to coat it, and add gently the remaining ingredients.

Bake in a greased and lined 8in (20cm) square tin in the middle of the oven at 300°F (gas 2) for 1½–2 hours. Leave in its tin for 20 minutes before turning out onto a wire tray.


## Gooseberry jam

4½lb (2¼kg) gooseberries
1½ pints (900ml) water

6lb (3kg) granulated sugar

Wash, top and tail the gooseberries and put them with the water in a preserving pan. Boil gently for at least half an hour until the fruit has softened. Add the sugar, stir until dissolved, then bring to the boil and boil rapidly until setting point is achieved. (Test this by putting two tabsp. into a cold saucer. Leave it in a cold place for 4 minutes: if when pushed the jam becomes wrinkled, it is ready.) Remove the scum at once, and leave the jam to stand for 20 minutes. Stir, pour into jars, cover with waxed paper and seal when cold.

## Strawberry jam

6lb (3kg) hulled strawberries
 (stalks removed)
12oz (375g) gooseberries
 (topped and tailed)

6lb (3kg) granulated sugar

Stew the gooseberries slowly in $\frac{1}{2}$ pint (300ml) water, simmering for at least $\frac{1}{2}$ hour. Mash the gooseberries. Put the strawberries, mashed gooseberries and sugar into a preserving pan. Heat gently with constant stirring until the sugar is dissolved, then boil rapidly until the setting point is reached. (See above for the test.) Remove the scum at once, and leave to stand for 20 minutes. Stir, pour into jars, cover with waxed paper and seal when cold.

## Marmalade

3lb (1$\frac{1}{2}$kg) Seville oranges
6lb (3kg) granulated or
 preserving sugar

5 pints (3 l) water
juice of 2 lemons

Wash the fruit and remove disc from stalk end. Halve the fruit and squeeze the juice. Put the pips in a separate basin and cover with 1 pint (600ml) of water. Slice the peel thinly and put it in a large mixing bowl with the fruit and juice and the remaining water. Leave to soak for at least 48 hours.

Put the fruit into the preserving pan. Strain the pips from the now jellified liquid in which they have been soaking. Tie the pips in muslin. Put all into the preserving pan. Cover and simmer for about one hour, or until the peel is quite tender. Take the pan off the heat. Add the sugar and stir until it is dissolved. Boil rapidly until setting point is reached (about 20 minutes). Take from the heat. Squeeze the muslin bag thoroughly against the side of the pan to extract all the pectin to return to the marmalade. Stir well. Leave to cool for 20 minutes before putting into clean jars. Cover with waxed paper and seal when cold.

# LANHYDROCK
*Bodmin, Cornwall*

## Luncheon for King George VI, Queen Elizabeth and Princess Margaret
*at Lanhydrock, 11 July 1950*

*Truite Saumonée*
*Sauce Verte*
\*
*Poulet au Riz*
\*
*Mousse aux Framboises et Framboises frais*
\*
*Cream cheese, butter and Cornish biscuits*
\*
*Peaches*
\*
*Coffee*
\*
*Sherry and Champagne pre-prandially*
*White wine, etc., during the meal*

## Salmon trout

12 peppercorns
salt
one tabsp. white wine

a bay leaf
1 tabsp. olive oil

Cook the fish whole in a covered pan with the above ingredients and enough cold water to come halfway to the top of the fish. Bring slowly to the boil and at once reduce, throwing in a little cold water if necessary to check the boiling. Simmer with very gentle bubbles for 8 minutes to the lb (18 minutes per kg), or finish when the bone will separate from the flesh when lightly prodded. Leave to cool in the liquid if to be eaten cold. Accompany with thinly sliced brown bread and butter.

## Aspic jelly

1 pint (600ml) fish stock
  (reduced by boiling from the
  above liquid)
1 glass white wine
2 egg whites

1 large tabsp. gelatine soaked
  in 2 tabsp. hot water
1 desp. tarragon or
  sherry vinegar

When the gelatine has absorbed the water, add it to the fish stock, the white wine and the chosen vinegar, and stir until it is dissolved. Add two egg whites, simmer for ten minutes and stir continuously until it rises. Strain through a scalded jelly bag until clear.

Garnish the fish with a simple decoration and spoon the aspic jelly over it on its serving dish.

## Sauce verte

yolks of 2 eggs
1 tabsp. tarragon vinegar
about ½ pint (300ml) best oil
2 tabsp. cooked and very finely
  sieved spinach

½ teasp. salt
a little pepper
a little cream
1 teasp. French mustard

Beat the egg yolks with the mustard and a little vinegar. When this begins to thicken, beat in oil (you may not have to use it all) very slowly until an emulsion begins to appear, then add the oil a little faster. Add salt, pepper, and the rest of the vinegar. Sieve the cooked spinach very finely, and add to the sauce with the cream.

## Chicken with rice

roasting chicken  
1 onion  

bouquet garni  
1 carrot  

Put the chicken to simmer either on the stove or in the oven at 300°F (gas 2) for about 50 minutes, with the onion, carrot, herbs and with water not quite to cover.

### Rice

6oz (180g) long rice  
1 whole onion  

about 1 pint (600ml) chicken stock  
salt  

Bring the chicken stock to the boil, add rice and onion and simmer for about 18 minutes on the stove or in the oven until the rice is tender. Add more boiling stock if necessary. Remove the onion when the rice is cooked.

### Sauce

3oz (90g) butter  
1 pint (600ml) strongly reduced chicken stock  
salt and pepper  

2oz (60g) flour  
2 egg yolks  
about 3 tabsp. double cream  
4oz (120g) mushrooms (optional)  

Cook the butter and flour together for a few minutes. Gradually add the chicken stock, boil for a few minutes and add salt and pepper. Beat the egg yolks with about 3 tabsp. double cream and add a little hot sauce. Return this mixture to the main sauce, and whisk over gentle heat for a moment or two to heat through.

Put the rice, with the jointed chicken on top, on the serving dish with the sauce spooned over the chicken. (4oz (120g) mushrooms, preferably buttons, cooked in butter, as well as a dash of lemon juice can be added to the sauce.)

Serve with small potatoes and peas.

### Raspberry mousse

1 pint (600ml) raspberry pulp  
6oz (180g) castor sugar  
juice of two lemons  

1 pint (600ml) whipped cream  
2oz (60g) gelatine  
3 eggs, separated  

Beat the egg yolks and sugar to a cream. Add the raspberry pulp, lemon juice with gelatine dissolved in it, whipped cream and lastly stiffly whipped whites of eggs.

Accompany with bowls of fresh raspberries and fresh clotted Cornish cream.

## Cream cheese

Set the cream with rennet, about 1 tabsp. to 2 pints (1200ml). Leave to drain through a fine cloth for 2–3 days.

## Biscuits for home-made butter and cheese

| | |
|---|---|
| 4oz (120g) flour | ½oz (15g) butter or |
| pinch of salt | 1 tabsp. cream |
| hot milk | |

Sieve the salt and flour together. Melt the butter in a little hot milk or add a little hot milk to the cream. Mix to make a dough, firm but soft. Either beat it with a rolling pin until it looks perfectly smooth, or knead it. Roll the dough out very thinly, cut into biscuits, prick them all over, bake on lightly greased tins in a hot oven for about 5 minutes at about 425°F (gas 7).

---

The luncheon party at Lanhydrock was for twenty, and it was an informal and light-hearted occasion, held in the dining room over-looking the delightful two-storeyed 1651 gatehouse and, beyond, the sycamores, some of which were planted as early as 1648. The flowers on the table were one of Queen Elizabeth's favourites, pink and white Malmaison carnations.

Miss D'Arcy, the housekeeper at Lanhydrock at that time and a highly qualified cook, received a personal message from the Queen saying how much they had all enjoyed the meal. An enlargement of a snapshot of the occasion, taken by one of the footmen, can be seen on the wall of the serving room. I am grateful to Miss D'Arcy for recalling and giving me these recipes.

Several factors contribute to the sense of welcome that one has on entering Lanhydrock, and an important one is that there are there people like Mr William Stephens, who has been employed at Lanhydrock all his working life—as were his father and grandfather before him. He served with the Guards in World War II, and apart from the war years has not been away; he is a Guide in the house he knows so well. It was Mr Stephens who put me in touch with Miss D'Arcy, now living in retirement in Yorkshire.

Mrs Evelyn Archer, the widow of Lord Clifden's valet and chauffeur, lives on the estate. She vividly remembers the occasion of this luncheon party. Mrs Archer remembers with great affection and happiness her life in the house and with the family:

These are some of my memories of Christmas at dear Lanhydrock, my home for many years. It really started on Christmas Eve. We were about twenty indoor staff. After the 6 o'clock news the presents for each one of us were all set out in the front Hall. We all had two gifts, one from the two Ladies and one from His Lordship. They were all bought in London when we went up in November for the Christmas shopping for about three weeks. We stayed at the London house, 7 Belgrave Square, and came back to Lanhydrock about ten days before Christmas. The butler found out from the men servants what they would like, and the Cook and myself what the maids would like. We each in turn when the bell rang went through to the front Hall to receive our gifts. The gardeners were given presents too.

Christmas morning started with Church at 8 o'clock, communion for those who wished it and back in the house for breakfast, and afterwards the gentry would come through to the servants' hall to see the huge Christmas tree, which the gardeners had brought in, and all the decorations the staff had done. Nothing was spared; it always looked a lovely sight (by the way, the servants' hall is now the tea rooms). 11.30 am we went to the morning service, and then the family had their lunch at 1 o'clock and we all sat down at 2 o'clock. There were always two huge turkeys and everything else to go with it, and the Christmas puddings were always alight when they brought them in. At teatime there was a wonderful Christmas cake and all nice things to eat, and suppertime cold beef and ham and mince pies, and we always finished up with games—nothing was spared, it really always was a wonderful day, and the gentry always made it as easy as possible for the staff.

New Year's Eve we also had goose for lunch (two), and New Year's Eve Captain Cecil, Lord Clifden's younger brother, always helped to ring the Old Year out and the New Year in with the bellringers, and they all came in the house afterwards for a drink and refreshments. I only want to say they were the happiest days of my life and they were wonderful people and not only to their staff but to anyone they could do a kindness to.

———

A fire in 1881 destroyed all of the old house except the detached gatehouse and the north wing. Nevertheless, an air of tranquillity is shared by the remaining 1640 fabric and the integrated later building, and all is intermingled with the air of a well-loved home.

Lanhydrock belonged to St Petroc's Priory, Bodmin, before the Dissolution. The sixty-acre Great Wood was first planted by the monks of the Priory, and Brownqueen Wood was the monks' deer park. There are superb views from the shrub garden beyond the Higher Garden on the slopes above the house. On a winter's day the wind through the great trees sounds like thundering surf. There are lovely walks to the river Fowey in the valley below.

The formal gardens near the house were laid out in 1857 by Sir Gilbert Scott. Bronze urns by Louis Ballin, goldsmith to Louis XIV, adorn these gardens.

The restaurant at Lanhydrock offers food in a comforting atmosphere, and is one of the increasing number of National Trust houses in Cornwall and Devonshire specialising in good cooking. The following is a selection of recipes, representative of the dishes offered.

———

## The National Trust Restaurant

### Beef in beer or wine

| | |
|---|---|
| 1½lb (720g) chuck steak | 8oz (240g) onions |
| 2 carrots | 2 leeks |
| crushed garlic clove | 2 sticks celery |
| bay leaf | pinch mace |
| oregano | thyme |
| touch of Worcester sauce (optional) | beer or wine |
| oil | seasoned flour |

Heat the oil. Coat the meat in seasoned flour. Fry the vegetables until golden and put them in a casserole with the herbs. Fry the meat until light brown and put with the vegetables. Add beer or wine scarcely to cover, and simmer for $2\frac{1}{2}$ hours on the stove or in the oven at 300°F (gas 2) or lower if simmering can be maintained.

Accompany with potatoes in their jackets (baked at the same time) and green salad.

## Fruit crumble

6oz (180g) self-raising flour
2oz (60g) Demerara sugar
1lb (480g) plums, stewed with
 a little sugar, or other fruit,
 such as fresh apricots or apples

3oz (90g) butter
pinch salt
2 teasp. arrowroot, blended
 in a little water

Prepare the fruit and drain almost all the juice onto the blended arrowroot. Put the fruit into an ovenproof dish. Rub fat into the flour, add salt and sugar and scatter over the fruit. Bake in a moderate oven for 20–30 minutes at 300°F (gas 2). Mix the juice and blended arrowroot and boil it to use as the sauce. Serve with Cornish clotted cream. (An alternative is to substitute quick-cooking oats for the flour. Mix the ingredients over gentle heat to blend, and proceed as above.)

## Tomato soup

$1\frac{1}{2}$ pints (900ml) well-flavoured
 stock which has been reduced
1lb (480g) fresh tomatoes or
 1 tin of tomatoes
1 pinch of basil
1 potato
2 slices of white bread,
 in small cubes, fried
1 carrot

2 small onions
2 lumps sugar
1 garlic clove, crushed
1 pinch of mace
salt and pepper
fresh basil
oil and butter to fry
cream (if serving chilled)

Slice the carrot, potato and onions finely and fry in oil and butter until golden. Add the rest of the ingredients except the bread croutons and the cream. Simmer until the vegetables are tender. Liquidise and sieve. Reheat and serve with the croutons (separately). If served chilled, add 1 spoonful of cream to each portion and sprinkle chopped basil over each.

## Leek and potato soup

1lb (480g) cooked potatoes
salt, if required, and pepper
chopped parsley stalks
1½ pints (900ml) stock

2 large leeks
1 rasher bacon, diced
oil for frying
pinch of mace

Lightly fry the bacon, then add potatoes and leeks and fry them until slightly golden. Add the other ingredients, checking in case salt is required. Simmer until all are cooked. Add hot milk if the soup is too thick. Use like this or sieve or liquidise. Serve hot, or chill and add cream and chopped chives. (The easiest way to clean the leeks is to cut from green and *almost* to root end twice, and then open them out to wash them.)


## Savoury flan with spinach and cottage cheese

### Pastry

6oz (180g) flour
3oz (90g) margarine and
   vegetable fat mixed

½ teasp. salt
1 egg yolk

Mix flour and salt, and rub the fats in. Mix egg yolk with one or two spoonsful of water and add to these. Roll out the pastry and lift into a flan dish, or simply press it neatly into a flan ring or dish about 9in (23cm) in diameter.


### Filling

1–1½lb (480–720g) spinach or
   11oz (330g) frozen spinach
a little single cream or top of the
   milk
1 clove of garlic
4 tabsp. grated cheese, preferably
   Parmesan; or anchovy fillets

8oz (240g) cottage cheese
1 egg and 1 white of egg
salt, pepper, cayenne pepper
pinch of mace
2 or 3 spoonsful breadcrumbs

Cook the spinach and sieve it. Press garlic juice into the spinach, add cottage cheese, egg yolk and cream, and mix with salt, peppers and mace. Stiffly whip the two egg whites and fold into the spinach mixture. Spoon the spinach into the flan pastry case, and either sprinkle cheese and breadcrumbs over it or arrange anchovy fillets and sprinkle the breadcrumbs over them. Bake at 400°F (gas 6) for 10 minutes, then reduce to 350°F (gas 4) for about 15–20 minutes. Eat hot or cold. (This flan will freeze well.)

## Cornish splits

1lb (480g) flour

1oz (30g) yeast or 1 level
    tabsp. dried yeast

¼ pint (150ml) lukewarm milk

2oz (60g) castor sugar

1 level teasp. salt

2oz (60g) butter or lard

¼ pint (150ml) lukewarm water

Mix four tabsp. flour with 1 teasp. sugar in a bowl. Add yeast to warm milk and water, and pour this into the flour and sugar. Leave for 20–30 minutes until frothy. Sift the rest of the flour, sugar and salt into another bowl, and add to this the yeast mixture with the softly melted fat. Mix it to a fairly soft dough that leaves the bowl clean. Turn it onto a floured surface and knead it until it is smooth and not sticky (about five minutes). Cover and leave to rise until double in size. Turn onto a floured surface. Knead lightly and divide into 14 equal-sized pieces and make into rounds. Place them well apart on lightly greased and floured baking trays. Cover and leave to rise until the dough feels springy when pressed with a floured finger, or for about 30 minutes.

Bake just above centre of a hot oven (425°F, gas 7) for 20–25 minutes. Eat hot, split open, with butter; or cold with Cornish clotted cream and strawberry jam.

# PARKE
*Bovey Tracey, Devonshire*

Bovey Tracey takes its name from the river Bovey and from the Tracy (later Tracey) family. One of the four knights who murdered Thomas à Becket in 1170 was William de Tracey of this parish. The parish church was dedicated at the time of the Saxon foundation to Saints Peter and Paul, and it is said that Sir William de Tracey rebuilt it as penance for his part in the murder. The Norman church was dedicated also to St Thomas of Canterbury, who was canonised in 1172. Some say that Thomas à Becket stayed at Parke, among other places, when he visited Buckfast Abbey and other foundations in the West country.

Parke was already beautiful in its park-like setting in Harold's time, and it is said that it was his favourite country house before he became king. There is a tradition that the Traceys lived at Parke, and that it passed into the possession of Sir William de Tracey at the beginning of Henry II's reign (accession 1154).

In 1826 Old Parke was demolished and a Regency house built on part of the site, but an impressive part of the earlier fabric remains.

The National Trust looks after Parke, but it is not yet open to the public. It was here that the BBC made the hilarious film *The Picnic*, with Ronnie Barker and Ronnie Corbett.

A kitchen book was started in 1876 by Mrs Hole, whose family later gave Parke to the National Trust, for her cook Blanche. The following menu comes from this book.

## Quenelles of fish

| | |
|---|---|
| 4oz (120g) uncooked white fish | 1oz (30g) butter |
| 1oz (30g) flour | 1 egg |
| salt, pepper, a little cream or milk | 2 egg yolks |

Melt the butter, add the flour, blend them and add a little water to make a panada or thick paste. Allow to boil and remove from the heat. *Either* (1) pound the fish in a mortar; (2) add the panada, 2 yolks and 1 egg, salt and pepper and a little cream or milk, to the fish and liquidise all together; or (3) pound all in a mortar. Shape the quenelles with two dessertspoons, place them in a large and shallow buttered pan with boiling salted water, and poach them gently for ten minutes. Makes about twelve. The recipe book suggests poaching them in 'small shaped tins' as an alternative method. When cooked lift them with a perforated slice on to a serving dish, and surround if liked with parsley or anchovy sauce.

## The Professor's curry

| | |
|---|---|
| a good handful of onions | 2oz (60g) butter |
| meat or chicken | 2oz (60g) curry powder |
| milk and lemon juice | salt |

Slice the onions and put into a stewpan with 2oz (60g) butter. Fry them until brown and take out of the butter. Cut what meat you intend to curry into small pieces, put them into the butter and fry them brown also. Take them out and put in the 2oz (60g) curry powder and fry until all the butter is absorbed. Return all to the stewpan and pour sufficient milk or water over the whole to cover it. Squeeze a little lemon juice over, add a spoonful of salt, and stew the whole very gently until all liquid is gone. It is essential that the curry should be cooked in a stewpan and not a frying pan. Accompany with chutney. Add sultanas to the curry if wished.

### Rice

Take best long-grained rice and put it into boiling salted water (2 cups water to each cup of rice). Boil for about 15 minutes or until a grain of rice is soft in its centre when pressed between finger and thumb. If more water is needed add boiling water, but not too much.

### Apple soufflé

about 1½lb (720g) apples          4oz (120g) butter
4oz (120g) sugar                  3 eggs, separated
juice and rind of 1 lemon (optional)

Cook apples in the minimum of water with flavouring. Sieve. Cream the butter, add the sugar, and beat again. Add apple purée and beaten egg yolks. Fold in stiffly whipped egg whites. Put into a lightly greased 2½ pint (1500ml) soufflé dish. Stand it in a baking tin with boiling water to come halfway up its side. Bake for about 30 minutes at 400°F (gas 6).

### Lady Abbess biscuits (or sandwich)

3oz (90g) sweet almonds pounded    4oz (120g) butter
2oz (60g) loaf sugar               a little rose water

Mix ground almonds, butter and sugar together with a little rose water until it all comes to a thick paste. Spread it fairly thinly on a well buttered tin and bake in a very slow oven for about 10–15 minutes. When cold, put a thin layer of preserve between 2 slices of the cooked paste and cut into thin strips with a very sharp knife. Arrange neatly in a glass dish or otherwise.

# ST MICHAEL'S MOUNT
*Marazion, Cornwall*

Celia Fiennes, the traveller and writer, visited St Michael's Mount in the 1690s and was made welcome. She was received by members of the family that is living there still. St Michael's Mount has been in turn a monastery (founded by Edward the Confessor (1003–1066), a fortress and, as it now is, a family home. 'The view of St Michael's Mount rising from the sea—"the great vision of the guarded mount" as Milton called it—is one of the most dramatic and moving things on our coast,' wrote the compilers of the *National Trust Guide*. The Castle's requirements are controlled by the weather, and Mrs St Aubyn described how 'the winter before last, our boatmen could only land twice in twelve days on the Marazion side!'.

'Perhaps,' suggests the *National Trust Guide*, 'the Saint chose one of the calm, scented summer nights of Cornwall for his dramatic appearance on the Mount one evening after dark in the year 495. Thenceforth at any rate the Mount was sacred . . . From the entrance to the castle, which bears the arms carved in granite of the first St Aubyn owner, to the extensive new buildings put up just over a century ago, the family has impressed its personality on one of the most unusual sites in England.' Withal, a home with a heart.

The Hon. Mrs John St Aubyn has kindly provided these recipes for luncheon, tea and dinner.

---

## Luncheon

### Haddock hongroise

4 haddock fillets and a
   squeeze of lemon juice
2oz (60g) mushrooms
scant 1oz (30g) plain flour

1 cup canned pimentos (optional)
1½oz (45g) butter
½ pint (300ml) milk
1 heaped teasp. paprika

Wash, dry and skin fillets. Place in a buttered fireproof dish and season with salt and a few peppercorns. Add lemon juice and water and cover with buttered paper. Poach in medium oven for 15 minutes. Slice mushrooms and place in a saucepan with half the butter. Cover and simmer for two minutes, then remove pan from the heat and drop in the remainder of the butter. When melted, stir in flour, paprika and milk and blend until smooth. Return to the heat and stir until boiling. Strain on the liquid from the fish and reduce for two minutes. Add drained cut-up pimentos, if used, for long enough to heat them through. Arrange the fish on a serving dish and spoon the sauce over it.

### Potatoes normande

1½lb (720g) potatoes
½ pint (300ml) milk
black pepper and salt

3 medium onions
butter
grated cheese (optional)

Slice potatoes *thinly*. Arrange in saucepan in alternate layers together with sliced onions, seasoning each layer. Add enough water to come half way up the potatoes. Boil till water has nearly evaporated and potatoes are cooked. Transfer to ovenproof dish and dot with butter. Grated cheese may be sprinkled on top. Cook in a slow oven for about ½ hour and brown under grill. Serve with green salad.

---

68

# Tea

## Cornish heavy cake

| | |
|---|---|
| 8oz (240g) lard | 8oz (240g) self-raising flour |
| 8oz (240g) sugar | 1 egg |
| a little milk | 8oz (240g) currants or mixed fruit |

Rub lard into flour. Add sugar and fruit. Mix to a dryish dough with the egg and milk. Spread on greased baking sheets. Bake in a moderate oven for about 30 minutes.

---

# Dinner

## Creamy carrot soup

| | |
|---|---|
| 1lb (480g) carrots | 3 onions |
| 1 pint (600ml) milk | 2 tabsp. butter |
| 1 tabsp. plain flour | black pepper, salt, nutmeg |

Slice carrots and boil them in salted water until tender; drain. Fry sliced onions in butter slowly until transparent (do not brown). Add carrots, more butter if necessary, and fry for a further five minutes. Draw aside, stir in flour to soak up the butter, pour in milk and mix well. Season. Return to heat and bring to the boil. Simmer gently for ½ hour till carrots are very tender. Cool slightly. Liquidise well. Return to pan, add a pinch of nutmeg and check for salt and pepper. If too thick, add more milk.

## Ragoût of lamb

| | |
|---|---|
| 2lb (960g) cooked lamb, chopped | 2 onions |
| 1 green pepper | tin of tomatoes |
| white wine (optional) | stock |
| 2oz (60g) butter | garlic salt, mixed herbs |

Fry onions and pepper in butter; add tomatoes and garlic salt with a few mixed herbs; simmer for five minutes. Transfer to casserole and add lamb and stock with wine. Heat for 30–45 minutes in the oven at 350°F (gas 4).

Accompany with boiled long-grained rice.

## Red cabbage

butter  
tablespoonful sugar  
wine vinegar

sliced onions  
shredded red cabbage

Melt some butter in a pan. Put in sliced onions and a tabsp. of sugar, which should burn a little. Put in shredded cabbage and simmer slowly with a little wine vinegar.

## Apricot mousse with Grand Marnier

8oz (240g) dried apricots  
whites of 4 eggs

3oz (90g) sugar  
2 tabsp. Grand Marnier

Cook the apricots and rub through a sieve. Add sugar, Grand Marnier and whites of eggs, stiffly beaten. Put in a soufflé dish to fill it well. Put dish in a pan of water and steam uncovered on top of stove for about 35 minutes. Transfer the mousse, still in the pan of water, to a slow oven for 20 minutes. If served cold, turn off the oven and leave mousse in to cool. No cream to be served with this.

## Savoury

Hot herring roes fried in butter, on toast.

## SALTRAM HOUSE
*Plympton, Plymouth*

The elegance of Saltram House is unassailable: however often Saltram is visited a pleasurable shock of delight recurs. The acoustic satisfaction of the double-cube Saloon remains 'audible' long after the visit—carry away in your imagination also the sheer beauty of the room by candlelight.

Saltram House is one of an increasing number of National Trust houses in Devonshire and Cornwall specialising in good English cooking. Saltram's kitchens aim to offer only fresh vegetables (the summer drought of 1976 caused acute shortages, and frozen peas had to be used occasionally as a supplementary vegetable), fresh meat, chickens and fish, as well as freshly-made soups and made-in-the-kitchen puddings, cakes and scones. The restaurant at Saltram House is established as a good place to come to because of the care and attention paid to the flavour and quality of its wholesome food.

*From The Countess of Morley, Buckland Monachorum, Devonshire (Saltram was the seat of the Earls of Morley until 1962)*

## Lettuce soup

2 large lettuces ('bolted' ones are quite suitable)
1oz (30g) butter
1½ pints (900ml) milk or milk and water mixed

2 teasp. arrowroot
1 medium sized onion, finely chopped
3 tabsp. thick cream
seasoning

Wash and slice lettuce finely. 'Sweat' onion in melted butter on low heat until transparent but *not* browned. Add lettuce and cover pan and leave on very low heat for 6–7 minutes. Add milk (or milk and water). Bring to boil and simmer gently for 20 minutes. Put the contents of the pan into the liquidiser and liquidise thoroughly. Return to the rinsed pan, add slaked arrowroot and bring to the boil stirring constantly. Add cream just before serving and check seasoning. (NB: This soup is equally good served really iced with cream added at the last minute.)

## Chops in puff pastry

6 neck cutlets of lamb or mutton
8oz (240g) packet frozen puff pastry
½ medium onion

2oz (60g) butter
salt and pepper
½lb (240g) mushrooms
1 egg

Trim meat from bone for one inch (2·5cm) from the top of each cutlet, dot with butter and grill for ten minutes, or until chops are tender, turning once. Leave to cool. Chop onion finely and slice mushrooms thinly. Melt butter in pan and 'sweat' onion until soft. Add mushrooms and cook till tender. Season.

Roll out puff pastry and cut into six squares and place a chop covered (on both sides if possible) with the mixture of mushrooms in the centre of each square. Wet edges of pastry and fold into a neat parcel leaving the sealed edges underneath and the bone sticking out of the top. Decorate with pastry 'leaves' made from rolled-out trimmings—two per chop. Brush with beaten egg. Place on a tray and cook in hot oven (425°F, gas 7) for about 30–35 minutes or until pastry is golden brown.

Serve with fresh vegetables in season.

## Orange caramel

| | |
|---|---|
| 8–10 juicy oranges | 6oz (180g) sugar |
| a little water | ½ pint (300ml) double cream |

Peel the oranges carefully with a sharp knife and cut away *all* pith and membrane. Holding the orange in one hand, carefully cut out each segment, leaving membrane behind—ie, cut down each side of each segment so that it comes out intact and minus skin (very messy and sticky, but well worth it). Place segments in glass dish with all juice available. (If at the end there is only a little juice, make a small quantity of sugar syrup and add this to the segments.)

### Caramel

Boil the sugar and water (about 6 desp.) together until the mixture is a light caramel colour. Pour half the caramel straight into the dish of oranges, and the rest into a tin and allow to spread to a thin sheet.

Before serving, whip cream stiff and crack the caramel on the tin so that it resembles broken glass—and then fold it into the cream. Place a dollop of this on top of the oranges just before serving.

This dish needs to be made in the morning and put in the fridge so that the caramel poured over the oranges has melted into the juices.

*Note:* Caramel is very easy to make provided the sugar is melted *before* the whole comes to the boil. Thereafter boil furiously until it starts to colour. Watch like a hawk: it quickly burns, and "dark" caramel is very bitter and ruins this dish.

---

Here are two party menus, used at Saltram in 1976 in the National Trust restaurant.

*Mushroom soup*
*Salmon mousse*
*Saltram casserole*
*Treacle tart*
*Sherry trifle*
or *Gooseberry and apple pie*
*with Devonshire cream*

## Mushroom soup

4oz (120g) mushrooms
1½ pints (900ml) chicken stock
nutmeg, pepper, salt
cream to garnish

1 small onion
1oz (30g) flour
2oz (60g) butter
chopped parsley

Fry chopped onion in butter, add sliced wiped mushrooms and fry lightly. Add flour, stir in and gradually add stock and seasoning. Simmer until the mushrooms are tender. Sieve or liquidise. Add a blob of cream and chopped parsley for each person.

## Salmon mousse

about 6oz (180g) fresh salmon
   or a tin of pink salmon
gelatine and stock, or aspic crystals

6 desp. mayonnaise
6oz (180g) tin Nestlé's cream

Mash salmon. Shake tin of cream before opening it, then mix the cream, salmon and mayonnaise. Melt aspic crystals in 1 pint (600ml) of hot water (or melt about ¼oz (8g) gelatine in 1 pint (600ml) of fish stock) and, when it is getting cold, mix into the fish mixture. Season and put into a soufflé dish, then into the refrigerator. Scatter chopped parsley over the surface of the mousse.

## Saltram casserole

2lb (960g) shin of beef
onion
pressed juice of garlic
oil for frying
seasoned flour

2 oranges sliced with skin
herbs, a little thyme and a bay
   leaf
red wine

Cut the meat into 2in (5cm) pieces, toss in seasoned flour and fry in a little oil until browned. Place all ingredients in a casserole with a lid, and cook very slowly in the oven for approximately four hours, at 250°F (gas ½). Serve with garden peas and creamed potatoes (beat the potatoes smooth with added cream, a little pepper and a scattering of nutmeg).

## Treacle tart

### Pastry

8oz (240g) flour
3oz (90g) lard or vegetable fat
a little water

2oz (60g) margarine
a little sugar (optional)
pinch of salt

Make the pastry using as little water as possible. Line a 5in × 10in
(12·5 × 25cm) tin with the pastry.

### Filling

2oz (60g) crushed biscuits or
  cake crumbs
6oz (180g) syrup, warmed

grated rind and juice of 1 lemon

Cover the pastry with the crumbs. Mix the syrup, rind and lemon
juice, and spread over the crumbs. Bake at 380–400°F (gas 5–6) for
about 25 minutes.

## Sherry trifle

6 eggs
3oz (90g) flour
5oz (150g) sugar
a pinch of salt

sherry
1 pint (600ml) milk
clotted cream

To make the sponge cake that forms the base of this sweet, whisk
three eggs and 3oz (90g) sugar until the lifted whisk leaves a trail.
Sift the flour well and fold it in. Put into two greased 7½in (19cm)
sandwich tins, and bake for about 15 minutes at 350°F (gas 4).

For the egg custard, beat three eggs and 2oz (60g) sugar together.
Boil the milk and pour a little onto the egg mixture, then add the
rest. Rinse the pan and return the custard to a very low heat: stir
constantly until it thickens enough to coat the back of the spoon
(instead of cooking on a direct heat, the bowl can be put in a pan of
almost boiling water). For hurried and/or preoccupied cooks, 1
tabsp. arrowroot, custard powder or cornflour can be added initially
to the eggs and sugar to preclude curdling.

Finally, soak the sponge cake in the sherry and cover with the
egg custard. Serve with Devonshire clotted cream.

*Salmon pâté*
*Devonshire chicken*
*Syllabub*
*Cheese, biscuits, celery*


## Salmon pâté

8oz (240g) cooked salmon          5oz (150g) unsalted butter
lemon juice                                    cream

Beat the butter to a soft cream consistency, mash salmon finely, and add to butter with lemon juice and finally cream, to make a suitable consistency. Serve with thin brown bread and butter.


## Devonshire chicken*

*for 8 people*

two 2½lb (approx. 1¼kg each)      7½ fl oz (225ml) white stock
   chickens or 8 joints                    6½oz (195g) butter
seasoned flour                            ¾ pint (450ml) cider
8oz (240g) chopped onions          1½lb (720g) dessert apples
7½ fl oz (225ml) double cream or  1oz (30g) flour
   evaporated milk                        parsley chopped for garnish

Cut chicken into 8 joints and dust each with seasoned flour. Melt 4oz (120g) butter and fry the joints until just golden. Lift the joints out and put in the chopped onions and half the apples, peeled, cored and chopped. Fry for 2–3 minutes without colouring, stir in the flour, add cider and stock and boil; then replace the chicken. Cover with a lid and cook in the oven until tender—about 40 minutes at 350°F (gas 4). Arrange on the serving dish. Reduce the sauce, add cream and reheat without boiling. Brown the remaining apples (sliced) in butter and arrange on the chicken. Pour the sauce over, and scatter parsley on top.

*The Devonshire Chicken recipe is taken from the West Country section of *A Taste of England*, which is extracted from *British Cookery*, edited by Elizabeth Boyd and published by Croom Helm. The book is the result of research commissioned by the British Tourist Authority and the British Farm Produce Council.

76

## Syllabub

*for 6 people*

| | |
|---|---|
| 2 desp. castor sugar | ½ pint (300ml) double cream |
| finely grated rind and juice of 1 large lemon | 4 tabsp. good quality brandy, wine or (dry) sherry |

Place the cream, sugar, grated lemon rind, strained lemon juice and sherry, brandy or wine in a mixing basin. Whisk together until quite thick, which may take a few minutes. Pipe with a rosette nozzle into six serving glasses. Decorate with a glacé cherry. Chill for several hours. Serve with sponge finger biscuits.

The Saltram recipe of AD1600 suggests whipping two egg whites stiffly, folding them into the syllabub and removing the froth to 'pile in your glasses as high as you can'; also, 'If you will have it of a red colour put in clarett instead of white wine, and a little at the bottom of the glass with a little sugar.'

---

The West Country Tourist board held a 'Taste of West Country' dinner in Saltram House on 30 March 1976. The food was from the West country, and so were the drinks.

The meal was: crab soup made from crabs caught off Porthleven, Cornwall, with Dorset Knobs from Morcombelake, Dorset; Torbay sole, delicately flavoured, perhaps the finest in Great Britain; and Wiltshire gammons prepared and cured at Totnes, Devonshire, baked with Dartmoor honey and Somerset apple and cider sauce, accompanied by minted new Cornish potatoes (dug that day) and buttered Devonshire broccoli spears. On a side table were such local specialities as Somerset and Devonshire syllabubs, Cornish burnt cream, apple cake, Devonshire and Cornish junkets, baked apple dumplings, Cornish saffron cake, Chudleighs, Bath buns, Cornish heavy cake, Wiltshire lardy cake. Then there were Cheddar and Dorset Blue cheeses with Bath Olivers and Cornish butter. The Cornish clotted cream used was prepared in the traditional way in the kitchen of the Bohetherick Farmhouse on the National Trust Cotehele Estate by Mrs Ernestine Cradick. There was Cornish mead from Newlyn and Coates' Plymouth gin, which has been produced at the Blackfriars Distillery at Plymouth since 1793.

The students of Mr W. Hirsch, a Lecturer at the Plymouth College of Further Education, Hotel and Catering Dept., presented this meal under his direction; and he has been kind enough to let us use one of the recipes.

## Strawberry and saffron shortcake

*Sweet saffron shortcrust pastry*

2 egg yolks
2oz (60g) castor sugar
6 teasp. water
10oz (300g) Cornish butter
strawberries

1lb (480g) soft plain flour
1 pinch powdered saffron
a little salt
whipped cream to decorate
clotted cream

(1) Mix together egg yolks, sugar and water.
(2) Sieve flour, salt and saffron in a bowl and rub in the butter.
(3) Mix gently into a firm paste with the egg, sugar and water mixture. Leave in a cool place for about 15 minutes.
(4) Roll out three rounds, 10in (25cm) across and $\frac{1}{4}$in (0·5cm) thick. Place on a baking sheet lined with greaseproof paper. Prick well with a fork.
(5) Bake in a moderately hot oven, 375°F (gas 5), for about 10 minutes. Make sure it stays pale brown.

When cooled out, fill with clotted cream and a plentiful supply of strawberries. Decorate with whipped cream.

# TRELISSICK GARDEN
*Feock, Cornwall*

According to the *National Trust Guide*, '... The earliest of them [the houses] were havens of comfort and security in a difficult and alarming world ... once the house was completed, there was little to tempt its owners and retainers to wander from it ... today it wears a less isolated look. Its park is a refinement of the surrounding fields, its lake the village pond writ large. Every visitor to Trust properties is familiar with the sudden tightening of the landscape which announces the neighbourhood of a great house. A wall or fence of unusual solidity bows inward to frame an entrance gateway, and there is a glimpse of fine trees rising from rolling grasslands, through which the unfenced road winds to the house ... Saltram, Antony, Trelissick ... all have parks of this type ... The English habit is to lead by serpentine approach to sudden display.'

The National Trust describes Trelissick Garden as 'a large garden, lovely at all seasons, with superb views of the estuary and of Falmouth harbour, [with] woodland walks beside the River Fal.' Mrs R. Spencer C. Copeland has recommended the following as a practical menu for a good summer luncheon in the garden. It can be quickly prepared, with a lot of the main preparation done well in advance. The quantities are to serve eight.

*First course*

## Ramekins

2 small tins pâté
  approx. 6oz (180g) each
2 packets Philadelphia
  cream cheese 3oz (90g) each

one 15oz (450g) tin beef
  consommé (Campbell's)
black pepper for seasoning

Put on one side a small portion of consommé to decorate tops. Place all ingredients in liquidiser, liquidise, and pour into small ramekin pots. Leave to set in refrigerator until required. Serve with garlic bread.

## Garlic bread

1 light loaf
pinch of salt

1 clove garlic
4oz (120g) butter

Set oven at 400°F (gas 6). Cut loaf, but not right through, into slices like a book. Crush garlic and salt and work butter in until creamy. Spread the garlic butter on either side of each slice, leaving some butter to spread outside. Press loaf back into shape, spread remaining butter on top and sides and wrap loosely in foil. Put in the oven for 15 minutes until crisp.

*Main course*

## Chicken fricassée

1 roast chicken (skinned)
½ pint (300ml) milk
4oz (120g) margarine
¼ pint (150ml) double cream

1 stock cube
pepper
4oz (120g) plain flour
2 tabsp. sherry or brandy

Dice chicken. Place milk and stock in a saucepan. In another pan melt margarine, remove from the heat and add flour. Return to heat, cook gently for one or two minutes and add milk and stock. Bring slowly to the boil, stirring all the time, and boil for three minutes. Allow sauce to cool. Add cream and sherry or brandy. Add diced chicken. Serve with green salad and orange and celery salad.

## Orange and celery salad

6 oranges                              1 good-sized head of celery

Remove peel and white pith simultaneously with a sharp knife. Slice the oranges. Cut celery into 2in (5cm) lengths and mix with orange slices in a bowl. Add vinaigrette dressing.

## Vinaigrette dressing

1 tabsp. sherry vinegar                3 tabsp. olive oil
  or orange juice           ½ teasp. salt
½ teasp. milled black pepper          fresh herbs chopped

Measure the oil and vinegar or juice into a bowl or screw-topped jar. Whisk or shake vigorously, then add seasoning and herbs.

*Sweet*

## Strawberry or raspberry gâteau

6oz (180g) plain flour                 pinch of salt
3oz (90g) butter                       6 eggs
6½oz (195g) castor sugar               1–1½lb (480–720g) strawberries
1 pint (600ml) double cream              or raspberries

The sponge can be made well in advance. Grease three 8in (20cm) sandwich tins, place a disc of greaseproof paper in each, grease again and lightly dust with castor sugar and flour. Warm the butter until it is soft and pourable—*not* until it is hot and oily. Whisk the eggs and sugar until the mixture dropped from the lifted whisk remains on the surface for a moment or two. With a metal spoon cut and fold two thirds of the three-times-sifted flour into the mixture, followed by the butter and then, quickly, the remaining flour. Fill the tins and bake at 350–375°F (gas 4–5) for 20–25 minutes.

Turn out the sponges and leave to cool. Prior to serving, whip the cream and place it and the strawberries or raspberries between each layer of sponge. Decorate the top and sides of the gateau with the remaining cream and fruit.

# CHRISTMAS DAY

*How will it dawn, the coming Christmas Day?*
*A northern Christmas, such as painters love,*
*And kinsfolk, shaking hands but once a year,*
*And dames who tell old legends by the fire?*
*Red sun, blue sky, white snow, and pearléd ice,*
*Keen ringing air, which sets the blood on fire,*
*And makes the old man merry with the young,*
*Through the short sunshine, through the longer night?*

*Or southern Christmas, dark and dank with mist,*
*And heavy with the scent of steaming leaves,*
*And rosebuds mouldering on the dripping porch;*
*One twilight, without rise or set of sun,*
*Till beetles drone along the hollow lane,*
*And round the leafless hawthorns, flitting bats*
*Hawk the pale moths of winter? Welcome then*
*At best, the flying gleam, the flying shower,*
*The rain-pools glittering on the long white roads,*
*And shadows sweeping on from down to down*
*Before the salt Atlantic gale: yet come*
*In whatsoever garb, or gay, or sad,*
*Come fair, come foul, 'twill still be Christmas Day.*

Charles Kingsley, 1868

82

The author of this Christmas poem, Charles Kingsley, was born at Holne Vicarage, Dartmoor. The Devonshire scenery here and at Clovelly in North Devon made a deep impression on his mind, and descriptions of it appear in his writings.

Here is a collection of recipes for really superb Christmas eating.

---

The description of this delectable feast, appeared, with coloured illustrations, in *Punch* on 17 October 1973, and Messrs Croft & Co., Ltd., the port and sherry shippers, have allowed me to include it in this book.

## The Edwardian Christmas Dinner
### *a gourmet's guide*

To begin. A dish of finest caviar. The addition of chopped onion and lemon juice is to be discouraged. Serve simply with thin slices of buttered rye bread and a glass of well chilled champagne.

After the caviar a tureen of game soup. To complement the flavour of partridge or hen pheasant a glass or two of Madeira.

Onwards. To poached fillets of brill, coated in a delicate shrimp sauce garnished with shrimp tails and sent to the table with melted butter. With this—a deliciously crisp Chassagne Montrachet.

Oysters. Served in the English manner with the juice of fresh lemons and, perhaps, a dash of cayenne pepper. After this a dish of mutton cutlets, grilled and placed on a dish around a mound of mashed potatoes and garnished with parsley.

Having thoroughly whetted the appetite we come to the zenith of the festive feast. A roast turkey. Garnished with bacon and sausages and served with bread sauce, or chestnut sauce or a good rich gravy. To drink? Claret.

To accompany the beauteous bird—a tureen of plain, boiled potatoes and a pyramid of buttered Brussels sprouts. Then to liven the senses what better than a dish of Russian salad? Not of the tinned and turgid variety so popular today. A genuine Salade Russe. Complete with truffles and mushrooms, French beans, beetroot, lobster, tongue and ham, mayonnaise et al.

A short respite and on to holly-decked plum pudding, with

brandy sauce or brandy butter whichever you prefer. For those with lesser appetites an alternative of maraschino jelly. For all, the luscious and incomparable Château Yquem.

To end. No bits of this and that. No meagre pots of cheese. An English Stilton. Ripe and round. With bread or biscuits. And celery—taken with a little salt.

The napkins lie crumpled. The cigars are lit. The port is passed from right to left.

Two ports represent the tradition since Charles II. Distinction. Very rare, very old, aged in the wood for ten years, sleek and tawny as a lion in sunshine. Commemoration. A fine vintage character, rich and full-bodied. As full of promise as the bride of Solomon.

The following are the authentic Edwardian recipes for what is, even today, a tantalising feast.

## Game soup

*for eight persons*

| | |
|---|---|
| 1 large pheasant or 2 partridges | 2 shredded onions |
| 2oz (60g) butter | 1 large carrot |
| 1 head celery | 1 lump sugar |
| 1 turnip | 2 quarts (2400ml) stock |
| salt and pepper | |

Cut into joints the bird or birds. Braise the pieces in the butter until tender, then take out the best joints and set them aside. Add to the remainder the onions, the celery and 3 pints (1800ml) of the stock. Simmer slowly for 1 hour, strain and take the fat off as cleanly as possible. Cut the flesh from the parts saved in neat pieces, and add with the sugar and seasoning; give one boil and skim again to have it quite clear. Simmer the cut-up carrot and turnip in the remaining pint of stock and, when quite tender, add to the soup. Time two hours. Bones and trimmings of game and the inferior parts of birds can be used to make more economical soup.

## Fillets of brill

Take amount of fish required, cut off the fins and clean the fish. Poach it gently in salted water, for 10–30 minutes according to size. Carve neat fillets, the thick part of the middle back being best. Coat in shrimp sauce.

## Shrimp sauce

¼ pint (200ml) melted butter
  sauce to each ¼ pint (150ml)
  picked shrimps
4oz (120g) butter
lemon juice

½ pint (300ml) milk and water
a little cayenne
2 heaped desp. flour
1 teasp. anchovy essence,
  if liked

Simmer the shrimp shells in milk and water, strain them and use the liquid. Melt the butter and blend in the flour. Gradually add the milk and water and bring to the boil, constantly stirring, to make a smooth sauce; cook for two or three minutes, add shrimps, anchovy and lemon juice and a few grains of cayenne. Still stirring very gently, heat through. Serve melted butter or melted butter sauce separately.

## Melted butter

2oz (60g) butter
¼ pint (200ml) milk

1 tabsp. flour
few grains salt

Mix butter and flour smoothly over low heat, gradually add milk and stir continually until it boils for two or three minutes. Add salt.

## Mutton cutlets

parsley to garnish
best end of neck of lamb or
  mutton (about 2lb (960g),
  5–7 cutlets)
1 egg
butter and oil

mashed potatoes
wine or cider to marinade
1 tabsp. oil to marinade
1 lemon, 1 bay leaf
breadcrumbs mixed with thyme,
  parsley and grated lemon rind

Prepare breadcrumbs and mix with chopped herbs and grated lemon peel. Leave the cutlets, which should be ¾–1in (2–2·5cm) thick, to marinade in the wine or cider and oil and bay leaf for as long as possible. Drain the cutlets, dip in beaten egg and then into savoury breadcrumbs, well pressed in. Brush well with melted butter and/or oil; grill under a hot grill for about seven minutes according to thickness, turning once. Make a pyramid of mashed potatoes and encircle it with the cutlets. Garnish with sprigs of parsley.

## Russian salad

(a)

| | |
|---|---|
| aspic jelly | 2 large red cooked beetroots |
| French or runner beans | artichoke bottoms, cut neatly |
| garden peas | small flowerets of cooked |
| asparagus tips |    cauliflower |
| | cooked firm potatoes |

Prepare enough aspic jelly to fill a border mould. Put some rough ice into a container suitable to stand the mould in. Cut the beetroot and potatoes into small columns of the size to stand round the inside of the mould, and drop them into liquid aspic jelly until ready to use them. Stand the mould in the ice and pour some aspic into it. Arrange diamonds of green beans, pieces of artichokes and peas on the aspic and run a thin layer over them. Take the small columns of potato and beetroot and arrange them alternately vertically round the mould, then fill the mould with aspic jelly.

(b)

| | |
|---|---|
| 2 tabsp. melted aspic jelly | salt and pepper |
| 3 tabsp. oil | 1 tabsp. tarragon vinegar |

Mix the above ingredients, and turn the remaining vegetables into the dressing. When required, turn the border out, and fill the hollow centre with these vegetables.

(c)

Into a bowl put a selection or all of the following: strips of lobster, anchovies, tongue, ham, prawns, sliced mushrooms, stuffed olives, a good tabsp. of capers, strips of lettuce, cress, sliced gherkins, chopped parsley, and all turned in a mayonnaise dressing (1 egg yolk, $\frac{1}{8}$ pint (75ml) or a little more oil, and lemon juice or vinegar), preferably coloured red with lobster coral.

Pile the mayonnaise mixture in pyramid fashion on the vegetables in the centre of the ring. Ornament the base with brightly coloured shapes of aspic jelly. Garnish with truffles.

## Maraschino jelly

| | |
|---|---|
| 4 tabsp. maraschino liqueur | juice of two lemons |
| 4oz (120g) sugar | 1$\frac{1}{2}$oz (45g) gelatine |
| 1$\frac{1}{2}$ pints (900ml) water | 2 whites and two washed shells |
| |    of eggs |

Put all except the maraschino into a large saucepan over gentle heat and whisk the mixture at once, continuing until it is almost boiling and there is a thick froth. Stop whisking, allow the froth to crack, and reduce the heat. Simmer very gently for a few minutes. Scald a jelly bag and pour the contents into it, over a basin. The jelly can be filtered twice. Finally add the liqueur and pour into a wetted jelly mould to set.

---

These four Christmas recipes are from Eliza Acton's *Newly Revised and Much Enlarged Edition of Modern Cookery For Private Families* (Longman, Green, Longman and Roberts, 1861).

## The Elegant Economist's pudding

Butter thickly a plain mould or basin, and line entirely with slices of cold plum or raisin pudding, cut so as to join closely and neatly together; fill it quite with a good custard; lay, first a buttered paper, and then a floured cloth over it, tie them securely, and boil the pudding gently for an hour; let it stand for ten minutes after it is taken up before it is turned out of the mould. This is a more tasteful mode of serving the remains of a plum-pudding than the usual one of broiling them in slices, or converting them into fritters.

## Eliza Acton's Christmas pudding

3oz (90g) flour
6oz (180g) beef-suet chopped small
6oz (180g) well-cleaned currants
5oz (150g) sugar
half a teasp. nutmeg and mace
  mixed (the mace pounded)
a small glass of brandy
3 whole eggs

3oz (90g) fine lightly-grated
  breadcrumbs
6oz (180g) raisins, weighed after
  they are stoned
4oz (120g) minced apples
2oz (60g) candied orange rind
a very little salt

Mix and beat these ingredients well together, tie them tightly in a thickly floured cloth, and boil gently for three and a half hours. We can recommend this as a remarkably light small rich pudding: it may be served with German, wine or punch sauce.

## German pudding sauce

¼ pint (150ml) sherry or Madeira     about 2oz (60g) sugar
yolks of three eggs     2 teasp. lemon juice

Dissolve the sugar—preferably castor—in the wine, warming it gently, but do not allow it to boil; stir it hot onto the well-beaten yolks of three eggs, and mill the sauce over a gentle fire until well thickened and highly frothed. Pour it over a plum or other sweet pudding, of which it much improves the appearance. We recommend the addition of two teasp. lemon juice to the wine. It is customary to froth sweet sauces in Germany with a small machine made like a chocolate mill. Two silver forks may be used in an emergency.

## Pre-Christmas pudding

(*Herodotus' Pudding, a Genuine Classical Receipt*)

Prepare and mix in the usual manner one pound of fine raisins, stoned, one pound of minced beef-suet, half a pound of bread-crumbs, four figs, chopped small, two tabsp. of moist sugar (honey), two wineglassfuls wine (sherry) and the rind of half a large lemon, grated. Boil the pudding for fourteen hours.

   Obs.—This receipt really is to be found in Herodotus. The only variations made in it are the substitution of sugar for honey, and sherry for the wine of Ancient Greece ... an accomplished scholar has had it served at his own table ... on more than one occasion ... we have given it on his authority without testing it; but we venture to suggest that *seven* hours, would boil it sufficiently.

---

The following recipes are from *Anne Andrews her Book*, a manuscript recipe book begun in 1756. It is a beautifully written and indexed record, and her descendant, Mary Lewis of Exeter, has been kind enough to allow me to use it. Anne Andrews was a granddaughter of the Robert Andrews in Gainsborough's famous picture.

## Plum pudding

1lb (480g) raisins stoned
1lb (480g) suet
7 tabsp. flour
4 fl oz (120ml) cream
citron and orange peel

1lb (480g) currants
6 eggs*
2 tabsp. brandy
mace, nutmegs, cloves, pounded

Mix and boil four hours ('4 *days* wd be better'—an added contemporary comment).

*Eggs were smaller then.

## Plum pudding
(a few years later)

½lb (240g) flour
½lb (240g) currants
3 or 4oz (90–120g) sugar
a little nutmeg

½lb (240g) suet
½lb (240g) raisins
4 eggs

(4oz (120g) breadcrumbs and 4oz (120g) flour may be used instead of the 8oz (240g) flour.)

Chop the suet very fine, and first beat the eggs well in a bowl; then add the flour, crumbs and suet and beat them all well, then grate in the nutmeg and add the other ingredients: if not moist enough add a spoonful or two of milk: dip the pudding bag in *hot* water, wring it out, flour it, and pour in the pudding. Boil it 3 or 4 hours. ('Or steam 6–7 hours, and when re-heating, 1½ hours'—later note.)

## Mince pies from Anne Andrews her book

3lb (1kg 450g) suet cut very fine
2lb (960g) currants, nicely pick'd, wash'd, rubb'd and dried by the fire
½lb (240g) fine sugar pounded fine
½ pint* (240ml) of brandy
½ pint* (240ml) of sack

2lb (960g) raisins stoned and chopped very small
half a hundred of fine pippins, pared, cored and chopp'd small
¼oz (7·5g) mace
¼oz (7·5g) cloves
2 large nutmegs, all beat fine

Mix all well together and put it down close in a stone pot, and it will keep good 4 months. When made into pies put citron and orange peel.

## Mincemeat

(a few years later)

3lb (1kg 450g) apples  
1½lb (720g) raisins  
1½lb (720g) sugar  
¼oz (7·5g) each mace, cinnamon,  
    cloves  
the rinds and juice of 2 or 3  
    lemons  
¼ pint* (120ml) Port Wine

1½lb (720g) suet  
1½lb (720g) currants  
a little salt  
1 pint* (480ml) brandy  
plenty of preserved lemon,  
    orange and citron & orange  
    marmalade

Prepare fruit and mix all well. Cover closely to store.

*An English pint was 16 fl oz until 1824.

## Lemon cheesecakes

Take the peels of three lemons—boil them in three different waters till they are quite tender, then beat them in a mortar with a quarter of a pound of fine sugar, the yolks of six eggs, ½lb fresh butter, the juice of ½ lemon and a glafs of good white wine; mix them well together, and put a paste at the bottom of yr pans, filled half full, and bake them about 20 minutes.

    Ingredients for the above:

3 lemons  
6 eggs  
juice of ½ lemon  
pastry

4oz (120g) sugar  
8oz (240g) butter  
1 glass of good white wine

Wipe the lemons thoroughly. Either use stored peels from previously squeezed ones or squeeze the juice from them. Keep the drained water after the three boilings (for a bitter-lemon drink). Boil the lemon skins until tender. Drain, add sugar and mash them very finely with a silver fork, adding the yolks and butter, lemon juice, a very small pinch of salt if necessary, and the wine. Beat until smooth. Leave for an hour or so if possible, to become thick and for the flavours to amalgamate.

    Line patty pans with pastry, fill half full, and bake for roughly 20 minutes at about 375°F (gas 5).

    Some of this mixture could be added to curd or cottage cheese to make a flan filling, with stiffly whipped whites of eggs folded in, and some currants previously marinaded in a little wine.

**Plum Pudding**
(about 1860)

3 fine apples chopped fine ¾lb (360g) plums (raisins)
¾lb (360g) beef suet 6oz (180g) currants
6oz (180g) flour 6oz (180g) sugar
2oz (60g) candied peel 2 well beaten eggs
½ nutmeg milk

Mix well together with sufficient milk to moisten it. It cannot be boiled too long.

---

The following two recipes for creams are from *Cre-Fydd's Family Fare*, published by Simpkin, Marshall and Co., London, 1864. This is a delightful cookery book, lent to me by Captain and Mrs H. P. Chichester Clark of Tavistock, and used in Captain Chichester Clark's north Devon family home.

**Brandy cream for puddings**

3oz (90g) loaf sugar 1 gill (150ml) good cream
a wineglassful of brandy

Dissolve the loaf sugar in a wineglassful of water; boil till in a clear thick syrup; then beat it into a gill of good cream; add, by degrees, a wineglassful of brandy. Serve over the pudding.

**Victoria sauce for puddings**

Dissolve 3oz (90g) of loaf sugar in a wineglassful of water; boil till a syrup; then add, whisking rapidly, the yolks of three fresh eggs beaten with a gill (150ml) of cream; and a wineglassful of brandy. Serve at once. (Note: the sauce should have the appearance of a rich smooth cream.)

**Lemon sauce**

Boil 3oz (90g) of loaf sugar and the thin rind of a lemon in a gill of water for a quarter of an hour; then add the strained juice of a lemon and two tabsp. of gin; strain and serve.

## Mincemeat

4oz (120g) raisins
8oz (240g) currants
4oz (120g) suet or melted butter
  or other fat
1 lemon
4oz (120g) almonds
½ teasp. each ginger, cinnamon
  powdered cloves
2 tabsp. brandy or sherry

4oz (120g) sultanas
4oz (120g) mixed peel
8oz (240g) apples
2oz (60g) brown sugar
½ grated nutmeg
¼ teasp. mixed spice
5 fl oz (150ml) rum

Stone and chop the raisins and place in a bowl, with washed and well dried sultanas and currants. Add peel, suet or other fat. Peel and chop finely the apples, grate the lemon rind and strain the juice and add. Add sugar, almonds, spices and the brandy or sherry and rum. Mix well, pot and cover closely.

---

## Christmas pudding

This is a delicious old and well tried recipe, coming originally from Jersey. Mrs Kenneth Rowe has been kind enough to allow me to reprint it from my earlier collection, *Devonshire Flavour*.

1 sherry-glass brandy
1lb (480g) stoned prunes
1lb (480g) shredded beef suet
1lb (480g) stoned raisins
1lb (480g) currants
finely grated rind and juice of lemon
6 eggs

4oz (120g) plain flour
½ teasp. each of mixed spice,
  grated nutmeg and salt
1 apple finely chopped
4oz (120g) mixed peel
2oz (60g) sweet almonds

Mix all dry ingredients. Beat eggs. Add all chopped fruits and nuts to flour. Make a well in the centre of the ingredients and gradually add eggs, stirring until all is very thoroughly mixed. Finally add lemon juice and brandy and stir thoroughly. Butter two large pudding bowls, fill and tie first with greased greaseproof paper, then with cloth. Steam 10 hours. Put clean cloths on when cold Steam 2 hours on the day required.

---

Francatelli, sometime chef to Queen Victoria, writing in 1846 observed that the English cooks pronounce 'petits-choux' as 'petty-shoes'. In spite of that he also wrote at that time that 'although bearing a foreign name he (the Author) is happy in being an Englishman'. These two recipes are from his book *The Modern Cook* (1860 edition), lent to me by Captain H. P. Chichester Clark in whose home in North Devon it had been since its publication.

## Petits-choux

½ pint (300ml) milk or water
2oz (60g) sugar
2–3 small eggs
a very little salt

4oz (120g) butter
5oz (150g) strong flour*
a few drops of essence of orange
2oz (60g) chopped almonds

Put the water, butter, sugar and salt into a stewpan on the fire, and as soon as these begin to boil, withdraw the stewpan from the fire, and add the flour; stir the whole well together with a wooden spoon over the stove-fire for about three minutes; by which time the ingredients should present the appearance of a soft compact paste. The essence of orange (or any other kind) should now be added, and also one egg; incorporate these with the paste, then mix in the other two eggs, and if the paste should be stiff, another egg or a yolk only, may be added. This paste should now be laid out on a baking-sheet (lightly greased) in small round balls, the size of a pigeon's egg, egged over with a paste-brush, some chopped almonds (mixed with a spoonful of pounded sugar, and a very small quantity of white of egg), strewn upon them, with some sifted sugar shaken over, and then baked of a very light colour. Bake for about 30 minutes, 425°F (gas 7), though they may take less than that. These may be served plain, or garnished inside with cream or some kind of preserve.

*Flour millers sell a strong plain flour especially milled for home breadmaking. They recommend it for Yorkshire puddings and for the rich pastries such as flaky, rough puff and puff and choux pastry. Ordinary flour, which is about 80% soft, is more suitable for other sorts of baking. A large proportion of our strong flour comes from Canada, where a shorter, hotter growing season produces less starch, but similar protein in the grain. This gives over 12% protein, compared with the approximately 9% of our soft flour. The two proteins that are present in flour are together described as gluten. The more gluten present, the higher the preparation rises in a hot cooking temperature.

## Spanish puffs

fat for frying                            foolscap paper

Prepare the petits-choux paste. Take a sheet of foolscap paper and
cut it into four pieces, spread these with butter, and then take up as
much of the paste as will stand in a small teaspoon; press it in
rows on the paper in the form of small round balls: this should be
done just before frying them. When about to send to table, take
hold of the sheets of paper containing the puffs, at one corner, and
as they are immersed in the hot hog's lard, shake them gently off
the paper; fry them of a light colour and when done, drain them
on a wire sieve covered with paper to absorb any grease: some fine
sugar must then be shaken over them, previously to their being
dished up on a napkin, in a conical form.

(A sauce can be handed separately, made from apricot jam or
apricot purée, mixed with hot water and grated lemon rind, blended
with a little arrowroot and boiled for a moment or two, until clear.
Add an orange liqueur if liked.)

# INDEX

95